THE MINNESOTA LIBRARY ON STUDENT PERSONNEL WORK

EDITED BY E. G. WILLIAMSON

* Published before titles were assigned numbers.

THIS IS VOLUME NINE
IN THE MINNESOTA LIBRARY ON STUDENT PERSONNEL WORK

. . . .

DECISIONS FOR
TOMORROW

. . . .

*Plans of High School Seniors
for after Graduation*

RALPH F. BERDIE and ALBERT B. HOOD

UNIVERSITY OF MINNESOTA PRESS, MINNEAPOLIS

Foreword

EACH answer we find to a previous question breeds new questions. The questions delineated by Dr. Berdie and Dr. Hood in this volume emerged from answers uncovered in the early research of Dean J. B. Johnston, Professor D. G. Paterson, and many others at Minnesota. The early questions essentially were "Who should be encouraged to attend college?" "Who should be admitted to and excluded from college?" "Who goes to college?" Since 1914, studies of student success and failure and descriptions of student characteristics have provided some answers to these questions. Enrollment figures indicate the extent to which college attendance has increased during this century. Through research we have found that increases in enrollment have *not* been at the expense of quality, that academic success in higher education can be predicted, and that college attendance itself is both predictable and understandable.

In the 1930's and 1940's, G. L. Anderson, T. J. Berning, and R. J. Keller continued the earlier Minnesota studies of college attendance. In 1950, Ralph Berdie provided a description of the plans and characteristics of the entire population of high school graduating seniors in the state. This study yielded not only statistics on the proportion of students who planned on and actually attended college, but other interesting information such as the percentage of high school graduates with fathers who were also high school graduates, the percentage with mothers who were employed, and the percentage with television sets in their homes.

More than anything else, this 1950 study revealed the complexity of student motivation. Dr. Berdie concluded: "The forces influencing the decisions of the 25,000 boys and girls we studied are complex and present a puzzle of causal relationships. . . . Whether or not a high school graduate attends college depends in large part upon the home from which he comes. The attitudes of the family toward things related to education, as shown by the books and magazines in the home, the community organizations in which the family is represented, and the education of the parents, are perhaps even more important than the family's financial resources. Children learn from their parents attitudes that may determine whether they want to attend college. Obviously if more qualified high school graduates are to attend college, any program of action must take into consideration the influence exerted by the family. Any program if it is to be effective in increasing the number of qualified students who attend college must attempt to influence the attitudes of both students and parents, as well as to reduce the economic barriers."

The study of 1961 Minnesota high school graduates reported here in a sense repeats the 1950 study but also extends and expands it. In recognition of the findings in the 1950 study concerning the importance of attitudes and values, this more recent analysis has taken into careful consideration many of the attitudes and personality characteristics of students as they are related to post-high-school plans. The earlier study showed that some students of high ability coming from the homes of skilled tradesmen attended college and some did not. The more recent study attempts to identify further distinctions between those who do and those who do not attend college; for example, evidence suggests the importance of student attitudes toward authority and toward social relationships.

Studies such as these are most important because they provide benchmarks necessary for the understanding of societal changes in education. Seldom is it possible to observe or evaluate experimentally developments in higher education. Descriptions of status and relationships in education become increasingly meaningful when appropriate benchmarks can be compared. Such benchmarks, for instance, help us to understand the increases in college enrollment from the early 1930's to the early 1960's. Similarly, the relationship today between college attendance and family economic status is better understood in light of the similar relationship observed a decade earlier. Certainly, some small reassurance may be gained from the knowledge that college attendance today is slightly less dependent on family economic status and slightly more dependent on student ability than it was in the past.

The studies completed in the Student Counseling Bureau at the University of Minnesota by Dr. Berdie and Dr. Hood have two other implications. First, it is clear that much meaningful educational research can be accomplished only by cooperative effort. The 1961 study was supported by the U.S. Office of Education Cooperative Research Program; it also received invaluable aid from organizations in the state: the Minnesota High School–College Relations Committee, the Minnesota Counselors Association, and the Minnesota Association of Secondary School Principals. In addition almost every high school principal and counselor in Minnesota was actively engaged in the collection of the necessary data. The basic test data for the study were available only because of cooperation over many years by Minnesota colleges and high schools in the Testing Program sponsored by the Association of Minnesota Colleges. Second, research such as this is most effectively accomplished in the setting of a continuing and successful service program that has engendered confidence in the persons to be involved in the research. Many efforts have been made to build into testing and counseling programs in Minnesota a research orientation, and those working in these programs have been encouraged not only to cooperate with specialists conducting research but also to engage in research themselves.

After completing a research report, the reader frequently asks, "Now what?" The study reported here leaves little doubt that if educational and counseling goals are to be achieved, certain things must be done. For example, adequate financial aid must be provided to students contemplating college, but financial aid alone is not sufficient. Students need individual counseling if they are to make wise decisions for their post-high-school careers, and high school and college counselors must direct many of their efforts toward the families of their students. The attitudes and values that help determine college decisions are formed long before the senior year in high school; assistance to students must begin early in their school years and be continuing and persistent.

Dr. Berdie and Dr. Hood have answered many questions, but they, like their predecessors, conclude by asking more questions than they have answered. Thus the field of educational research concerning this complex of questions and research problems requires still further research studies.

E. G. WILLIAMSON
Dean of Students and Professor of Psychology

July 1965
University of Minnesota

Acknowledgments

THE climate of splendid cooperation in secondary and higher education in Minnesota has enabled educators in the state to learn much about their students and their schools. This study of the plans of high school seniors essentially is part of the State-Wide Testing Program supported by the Association of Minnesota Colleges and touching every college and high school in the state.

The authors deeply appreciate the cooperation of the Minnesota High School–College Relations Committee, which jointly represents the Association of Minnesota Colleges and the Minnesota Association of Secondary School Principals, and certainly they are grateful for the endorsement of this study by the Minnesota Counselors Association.

The high school principals and counselors in more than 500 public and private schools in Minnesota aided the study by administering the questionnaires, thus continuing their long tradition of cooperation in the State-Wide Testing Program. Most importantly, the cooperation of the more than 46,000 high school seniors who graduated in Minnesota in 1961 must be acknowledged. This study, and subsequent ones, have made this group of seniors perhaps the most studied state-wide group of high school students in Minnesota's history.

Many individuals helped plan and conduct the study. Dean E. G. Williamson has provided strong support and great wisdom to the authors. Dr. Edward O. Swanson of the Student Counseling Bureau has facilitated in many ways their use of the test data. Emily Dawson, Gary T. Athelstan, Anna M. Tollefson Sollid, Bruce D. Grussing, Dianne D. Ziskin, and David L. Seaquist were graduate research assistants who did much of the analysis and provided many helpful suggestions.

Sharon L. Higgins MacPhail and Mary Ann Latvala Johansson were undergraduate research assistants who devoted several years to this research project as "Jills-of-all-trades." Douglas L. Elliott and Robert I. Flynn worked on the data-processing and computer-programming aspects of the study. Charlene E. Barrett, Monica M. Birdsall, Donna M. Jones, Elizabeth B. Knaff, Sherrie L. Vaughn, and Sandra M. Zinkin did the vast amount of tabulating and keypunching of the information necessary before the results of this study could be analyzed. Nellie D. Boyce, Carol Ann Lee, and Linda Rogers did all of the clerical work and coding in translating this material from questionnaires to IBM cards. Constance A. Tyson Hagen typed much of the final manuscript.

Appreciation is also expressed to the U.S. Office of Education of the Department of Health, Education, and Welfare for the financial support which made this study possible through Cooperative Research Project No. 951–(SAE-8976).

R. F. B.
A. B. H.

July 1965
University of Minnesota

Table of Contents

DECISIONS FOR TOMORROW

Attitudes, Behaviors, and Plans of High School Seniors

WHAT are the plans of high school seniors? What determines these plans? These two questions are often asked by students, parents, teachers, counselors, and by government and social planners. The well-planned high school organization and curriculum must therefore take account of the objectives and possible future behavior of graduates. In specialized high schools, students are grouped in particular curriculums according to their educational and vocational objectives; the student who has not yet formed any definite objectives more or less arbitrarily adopts one of the available curriculums, perhaps on the advice of his parents, or he may be assigned to one that seems suitable by the school itself. In the comprehensive high school, students may be assigned to special curriculum groups within the school or may be advised to follow individually planned curriculums, with selection of program depending on their post-high-school objectives. The comprehensive high school, particularly the larger ones, may offer differentiated curriculums, but since almost 80 per cent of American public high schools have fewer than 100 students in the senior class, most schools obviously cannot support highly differentiated curriculums (Flanagan, *et al.*, 1962).

Whether students are assigned to special curriculum groups or are helped by the school to select individualized and appropriate courses and programs, the effectiveness of differentiation depends upon the school's having adequate knowledge of the student's objectives and of the influences determining his decisions.

Education after high school is differentiated to an even greater extent

3

than secondary education. What a terminal junior college attempts to do with its students differs in many ways from what is attempted by a four-year liberal arts college. A post-secondary technical training school is concerned with many kinds of student development that are of no concern to the teacher-training institution. Although some general objectives may be shared by most or all post-secondary schools, an outstanding characteristic of these schools is the extent to which they seek to provide a variety of educational programs. Such schools depend greatly on their knowledge of student purposes and objectives and of the determinants of these objectives. A post-secondary school assumes, as does a high school, that its students share certain needs and that, at the same time, individual students have unique needs; and the school attempts to meet both kinds of needs, usually by providing differentiated curriculums. Often an attempt is made to tailor a student's program to his particular needs. Again, regardless of whether students are assigned to existing programs or to special programs developed for individual cases, effectiveness of differentiation depends on the school's possessing adequate knowledge about each student's abilities and objectives.

Society at large — the general public, the government, business, industry, and education — has a great interest in the plans and decisions of high school graduates. Although somewhat predictable, manpower needs are often erratically defined and estimates of the national demand for differentially educated persons are affected by the biases and vested interests of the estimator, the definitions and categories employed, and the prevailing economic and social conditions. In spite of the precarious basis for such predictions, social planning and influence are sometimes necessary. When the best available evidence indicates a shortage of physicians ten years hence, the community must make efforts beforehand to ensure that future needs for medical personnel are met.

Although concern about manpower potential frequently is justified, every individual and group must be even more concerned about the general educational level of the population as a whole. Our civilization is based on mass education and, in spite of what some critics contend, on mass education of high quality. Since the country's inception continuing efforts have been made to increase the proportion of educated persons and at the same time to improve the quality of education.

This perhaps is the unique American development. Some nations in-

4

vest their educational funds in providing a small number of people with the best possible education, assuming that with competent and talented leaders the nation will develop and progress. The American assumption is that without well-educated masses, the efforts of leaders will be ineffective.

Under constant examination is our continuing assumption that leaders can be trained in the public educational structure that is available to all. Many persons think that special, separate educational programs are needed to develop potential leaders, that particularly talented and gifted persons require educational systems suited to their own needs. In contrast, others maintain that unique programs can be offered to individuals within a single system. If such a system can be devised, one that designs the education most appropriate for each person, separate systems may not be necessary. The success of many comprehensive high schools provides evidence supporting this view (Berdie, 1958).

The decisions of the high school graduate regarding his plans for the future necessarily involve his parents, teachers, and counselors. Students seldom know much about the process they have passed through in reaching a decision and know relatively little about the influences determining their plans, although many can present a brief and superficial explanation, and many can — to their own satisfaction — justify their plans. A surprising number of students who attend college will explain that their parents had nothing to do with this decision, that their parents constantly insisted that the decision was the student's and not the parents'. Many students are unaware of the more subtle influences exerted by the family.

Counselors can help students make decisions, and most students when talking with counselors reveal preferences for some alternatives over others. Part of counseling consists of helping students to learn more about their preferences and to decide which are valid. A basic assumption of counseling is that people who make choices should make informed choices and should know as much as possible about why they are so choosing.

Counselors are interested primarily in helping students make sound choices and in assisting them to understand their decisions. Parents, teachers, and many others in the community also hope that students will make sound and informed choices. Usually the principal interest of the parent or teacher is the welfare of the student. A parent may attempt to influence his child to decide to attend college because he believes that in the long run his child will have a happier life as a college graduate. Parents may be impelled by their own desire for status, perhaps by the hope that the economic success of their children will enhance their own status in the community and their own financial well-being, but most persons attempting to influence students to attend college are motivated by a sincere desire to help these young people.

Representatives from many social institutions and community organizations have an interest in influencing the decisions of young persons. Educational administrators hope that enough qualified persons will decide to become teachers. Every citizen hopes that enough young people will decide to enter necessary occupations such as medicine, automobile repair, and mortuary science. Representatives from industry hope for an adequate supply of engineers, accountants, personnel directors, and technicians. If too few persons are deciding to enter these careers, or if the wrong people are so deciding, these social agents then attempt to influence decisions so that an adequate distribution will prevail in the labor pool.

These were the reasons for undertaking the study described in this volume. Presumably counselors may benefit from studies of this kind and become more effective by learning more about the decisions made by young persons and the determinants of those decisions. It is also hoped that society in general may benefit from being informed about the factors that influence these decisions, that behavioral scientists may satisfy their curiosity and refine their theories with information so derived, and, finally, that students may be enabled to improve their self-understanding and their ability to make better and more appropriate decisions.

THE ACT OF POST-HIGH-SCHOOL DECISION

The educational or vocational behavior of a student immediately following high school graduation can be considered as a combination of specific attitudes and observable acts occurring within a definable situation. For purposes of convenience we will discuss attitudes and behaviors directed toward college, although the same approach can be applied productively to attitudes and behaviors directed toward other post-high-school objectives — employment, entering a school of nursing, starting trade or business school, or perhaps even immediate marriage.

The behavior here called "college attendance" consists of specific acts, which can in turn be analyzed or broken down into subordinate acts or steps in the entire process. For example, steps included in the act of attending college are (1) requesting and receiving an application for admission; (2) completing admission forms; (3) requesting personal recommendations; (4) requesting high school records for the college; (5) paying application fees; (6) submitting application forms; (7) reserving dormitory rooms or finding living quarters; (8) traveling to the college; (9) paying college fees; (10) registering for courses; (11) participating in orientation programs; (12) purchasing texts; (13) attending classes; (14) engaging in campus activities; (15) taking examinations.

College behavior as it encompasses these acts can occur only after the student has decided to attend college, a decision resulting from many conditions. In the present study we regard the decision to enter college as equivalent to the behavior of attending college and report evidence indicating the extent to which this assumption is justified. We shall discuss the decision or the plan to attend college as if it were the same as the behavior of attendance, recognizing the limitations of this assumption.

The influences affecting the decision to attend college can be categorized roughly as related to family, school, peers, and self.

Influences within the family include economic variables, cultural and educational variables, social and emotional relationships, and, for lack of a better term, family attitudes toward college. The complex economic variables, although summarized by referring to the total financial resources of the family, also depend on the financial demands the family must meet, its habitual pattern of spending and saving, the expectations and probabilities of future income, and family attitudes toward financial resources.

The cultural and educational variables are equally complex and include the amount and type of education of the father and mother, the reading, intellectual, and cultural habits of the family, the educational and intellectual attitudes and activities of groups and organizations to which the family belongs, and the intellectual and cultural community resources to which it has access.

The attitudes and emotional relationships within the family are related to the extent to which the student rebels against parents, authority, and social expectations, the extent to which he is docile and dependent on the opinions of others, the immediacy of his needs for complete — or what he regards as complete — independence, and his willingness to postpone the gratification of certain satisfactions in order to satisfy other needs.

The variables directly related to school influences include the student's satisfaction with his past school experiences and his emotional reaction to his current and immediately past experiences. Though a result of other experiences, satisfaction is an emotional condition often directly observable in verbal and other overt behavior that is significant in determining the decisions of the high school graduate. Another school variable can be labeled "stimulation." Though related closely to satisfaction, it includes more than satisfaction insofar as its chief expression is shown by an increased desire to learn. Other variables center on the adequacy of the school itself, in training and experience of teachers, in amount of money spent per pupil, in library, laboratories, and building, in curriculum, in activities program. Finally, one important variable, the counseling and guidance program, includes availability and quality of personal and vocational counseling, adequacy of personnel and guidance records, and extent of individualized and personalized attention given to students.

The variables directly related to the student's peers which influence his decisions for behavior after graduation include number and types of friends and associates, their attitudes, habits, plans, families, school experiences, and out-of-school attitudes.

Another perspective of these influences is gained when we look at them from the student's point of view. Decisions are influenced by the student's ability, which is a product of his organic and physiological constitution and his complete behavior history. Other important and complex variables are related to his needs and interests, variables that can be envisaged in many ways. His personal adjustment is another self-variable influencing decisions, adjustment to his peers and friends, to his family, and to his community.

In addition to family, school, peers, and self, other sources of influences determining post-high-school decisions can be identified that are related to the church, community groups, and the mass media of communications.

8

The decision to attend college is always a segment of a process. Sometimes the decision appears almost spontaneously, with the process being relatively brief, but usually the decision is merely the verbal enunciation which emerges from the process in its later stage. For many the process begins early in childhood; family, school, and peer variables are soon at work, influencing the student even before he begins school. In some cases the process is not really active until he has entered junior or perhaps even senior high school. Usually, for most students, influences determining post-high-school plans can be identified before the ninth grade. Although they are not terminated when the student finally makes his decision, or when he enters college, the behavioral manifestations resulting from these influences do change.

The decision of the student and his subsequent behavior are not only a result of the conditions described here but also a function of the alternatives available to him. If the probability of attaining an objective is so small that it is practically impossible, that objective cannot be considered as an alternative. For a child mentally retarded and unable to read or write, college is not an alternative. A paraplegic idiot has no educational or vocational alternatives. It would make no sense to talk about his decisions or about his choice.

Similarly, many high school graduates make certain decisions not as a result of choice among alternatives but rather as a result of limited alternatives.

The great increase in the proportion of high school graduates who attend college can be attributed in part to the gradually increasing educational level of the population, the greater availability of colleges, the greater awareness of the need for educational and vocational competence, and the increasing ambitions of children and their parents. Many students attend college, however, not as a result of any of these direct influences but because so few or perhaps no other alternatives are available to them. The largest proportion of high school graduates have IQ's ranging from 90 to 110. Many of these students have no great, or perhaps even observable, intellectual drive or curiosity impelling them toward higher education. Many of them have no economic or vocational goals that suggest the need for higher education. But at the same time many of them have no unusual aptitudes, abilities, or skills that encourage serious consideration of training or occupations requiring other

9

than academic education. Many of them have no alternatives other than college.

The average high school graduate such as we have been describing is restricted in opportunities to find a job that promises any kind of a future. Apprenticeship opportunities require certain specialized aptitudes that many do not possess, and are therefore available to only a few. Opportunities for on-the-job training are rare. Many young men enter military service immediately after graduating from high school with the hope that after release, when they are older, attractive jobs will be available to them. Many young women marry immediately after graduation and solve, or at least postpone, the problem of choice. An increasing number of young persons, however, are attending college because it has become almost inevitable that they should do so. They have not really made a choice, nor have their families chosen; they have simply taken the only road that seems to offer any probability of leading to some kind of fulfillment.

PERSONAL NEEDS

The determinants of post-high-school plans exert their influence on the student over a long period of time. In view of the complexity of these determinants and the duration of their effectiveness, student behavior becomes more understandable if the concept of needs is used. Needs are psychological conditions inferred to be present within the person, these inferences being based on his history, on his experiences and their effect on his subsequent behavior. Needs are concepts, not attributes of the individual, but as concepts they help describe the person — both the person as he is, as a result of his history, and as a potential doer of deeds.

The range and number of needs that can be conceptualized are almost limitless. A rather restricted number, however, appear to be most relevant to the planning of high school graduates. First is the need to do something, the need for action, the need to behave. Once a student completes his high school career, he can hardly cease existing; he must do something. Though doing something may consist of sitting at home looking out a window, we cannot question the inevitability of some behavior on the part of the student. The need to do something may be basic and underline all other needs. Discussions with many students

10

suggest that this is the most potent need in setting them on their post-high-school road.

The need for independence is often mentioned by students when discussing their plans. It is sometimes described as a need to escape an undesirable condition of dependency. Some students say the reason for going to college is to get away from home, to escape an overly strict mother or a demanding father. Some claim independence as a reason for going to work, to be free of having to ask someone else for every cent they need, free to associate with whomever they wish, free to "live the kind of life they want." For others this need for independence is expressed by a desire not so much to escape an unhappy situation, but rather to attain or reach a level they consider more mature, more appropriate for a young adult. Young girls living at home quite free from parental restraint and maintaining satisfying family relationships often move into apartments of their own or rooming houses because they consider this is the appropriate way for a young lady to live. Many students decide to move away from home when they attend college so they can test themselves, living on their own, assuming greater responsibility for their own actions, and facing crises and emergencies with only their own resources. The need for independence here is essentially a need to change a way of life, from a way considered appropriate for a child to a new way considered appropriate for an adult.

The need for security often influences student decisions. In contrast to the need for independence, fear of leaving home may prevent a student from entering a school, or from seeking employment, in another city. Although the need for financial security might influence one student to take a job in a new and strange situation, it might influence another to decide against entering college because of uncertainty about having sufficient funds. Those who define security as money in the bank, a down payment for a home, or a job with continuing income, will the more readily accept employment immediately after high school graduation. Others, who define security as a long-term objective, as establishment in a way of life requiring basic preparation, are better motivated to enter college. For each person, security is something different; perhaps every decision is influenced by the person's striving to attain security as he perceives it.

Need for status, recognition, and acceptance influences many of these

11

decisions. In making social beings out of squalling organisms, society relies most of all on social reinforcement. The approval and disapproval of parents, teachers, and peers may be the principal determinants of personality development. Certainly many students decide on particular post-high-school plans because these decisions win the approval of persons they value. A student's associates rarely agree on what is socially approved behavior. A boy's teachers and counselors may approve more of his attending college than of any other plan; his parents may prefer his seeking employment; and his friends may grant most status to associates who enlist in the Army. Students do not seek approval from a single source for their different activities. A student may derive satisfaction from reinforcement provided by a teacher for satisfactory academic performance and ignore the reactions of other students. On the other hand, he may rely heavily on the acceptance of other students for behaviors outside the classroom. When needs for status and recognition are discussed, consideration must always be given to the source of status, the behavior being acknowledged, and the conflicting values of persons from whom the student receives recognition.

All persons have needs for learning and for mastering skills, and for some these needs are important determinants of post-high-school plans. Stimulation from parents or teachers may result in wishing to learn more about literature or mathematics simply for the excitement and satisfaction such learning provides. Many students enjoy learning about new ideas and take pleasure in developing skills in analysis and evaluation. Many decide to attend college because they want to learn; many decide to take jobs because they want to become experts.

Finally, a need can be conceptualized that encompasses all the needs discussed here, a need for "role fulfillment." Essentially, this means that many persons have an idea as to the kind of lives they desire, the kind of persons they wish to be, and their behavior is strongly motivated by the need to attain these roles. Role fulfillment takes into account a person's ideas about independence, security, status, and competence, always relative to the roles of others about him as perceived by himself. Seldom is this role defined in detail by the student. He may have a vague, general idea that it encompasses, among other things, his being a college graduate. Asked what kind of lives they would like to lead, students give varying answers. A young man might say he wants a job that will allow him to live in a desirable area, to raise a family in a certain way, to travel to interesting places, to derive specific satisfactions from the kind of work he will do, to listen to preferred records and music, to read books and magazines, to participate in his hobbies, to have congenial friends, to assume social and community responsibilities. When a student says, "I want to be a lawyer," he usually means all of these things. When a student says, "I want to have an income of fourteen thousand dollars a year," he may mean all of these things. Most persons do not really see the roles they have defined for themselves until they are rather successfully playing or living these roles. Then a person looks at himself and his role and decides what his values are and how satisfying his life is.

THE FACTOR OF FORTUITY

A statistician reviewing the research on plans of high school graduates would decide that, to date, no more than 50 per cent of the influences determining these plans have been accounted for or identified. Knowledge of the abilities, family backgrounds, socioeconomic conditions, schools, and personality variables of high school graduates predicts college attendance no more than would be indicated by a multiple correlation coefficient of .70. This knowledge is limited because of, first, the inadequacy and incompleteness of our methods of observation, measurement, and analysis, and second, the fortuitous nature of the behavior studied.

Many decisions of high school graduates are influenced by accidental factors. A student living in an area where a sudden change in economic conditions causes most of the workers to lose their jobs is forced to give up his plans for college. Another, not planning on college, inherits three thousand dollars from a relative and decides he can go to college after all. Revision in policy of a student's Selective Service Board allows him to make new plans. Another young man develops infectious mononucleosis or tuberculosis and has to defer his plans until well.

Changes in the policies and organizations of the high schools themselves, or the establishment of a new college in an area, can significantly affect the plans of high school seniors. Economic conditions, climate and weather, health, transportation facilities, new emphases in newspapers and other mass communications media — all can seriously influence the decisions and behaviors of students.

These fortuitous factors are perhaps less important for students who have committed themselves definitely and for long periods of time to specific decisions. For many students, however, decisions are tentative and borderline. Many face alternatives that appear equally attractive, or equally unattractive, and the influences that determine the choice of one alternative over another are small, frequently almost unobservable. Many situations become so complex that the student cannot anticipate what will happen, nor can anyone else.

Elsa, when graduating from high school, decided to marry Donald, a boy with whom she had been going for several years. Donald was drafted, and the couple had to decide whether to get married immediately or after his discharge. Elsa decided to attend college for the eighteen months of Donald's service period, and he then decided that after service he also would attend college. Elsa then had to decide whether she should continue college or seek employment to acquire a nest egg so that the two of them could manage until he finished college, with provision for her attending school part-time and completing her academic work after he completed his. The international situation then changed, the policies of the Selective Service Board shifted accordingly, and Donald learned that he would not be drafted after all.

Each student faces a pattern of events and probabilities unique for him, and what we here call fortuity is simply the unique aspect of the determinants of plans. Because of this, our ability to predict accurately for the individual always will be limited, although increased knowledge and improved methods should allow great improvement in our ability to predict group behavior.

RELATED RESEARCH

The behavior of post-high-school planning has been studied for several decades and the literature on this subject is vast. A summary of the literature before 1954 was included in *After High School — What?* (Berdie, 1954), and a more recent summary of later studies was published in 1961 by the United States Department of Health, Education, and Welfare (Beezer and Hjelm, 1961). No attempt will be made here to review in detail the studies since 1954, although some will be briefly summarized and an attempt made to generalize from their results. The studies will be divided into three groups, first those restricted to particular states, areas, or regions within the United States, next those pertinent to Minnesota — the research reported in this volume being on Minnesota students — and finally research attempting to describe conditions in the entire United States.

State and Area Studies. Since 1950 significant studies of post-graduation plans of high school seniors, usually centering on plans to attend college, have been reported in Minnesota, Ohio, New Mexico, Montana, Indiana, Kansas, Kentucky, Arkansas, Wisconsin, Nebraska, Michigan, New York, and Illinois. Three general methods have been used to collect information in these studies: questionnaires given to students or parents, interviews with students or parents, and examinations of high school records and reports from high school personnel. Two types of information have been examined, that pertaining to the plans of high school students and that consisting of reports of the actual behavior of students — that is, not what they planned, but rather what they did.

The time at which information was collected varies from study to study. Although in some studies information regarding plans was collected early in the high school career of the student, it was usually collected during the latter part of the student's senior year. Information about actual behavior was usually collected within one year of the time the student graduated from high school, but occasionally at a later period. Sampling of students also varied from study to study. In some, information about all students in the state or area was sought. In others, random or representative samples were used. In still other studies information was collected only from students with specified abilities, high school records, residences, or sex.

Different conditions affecting high school plans have been observed, with some studies concentrating on only one or two related variables, others considering many variables. Almost all paid attention to the sex differences related to post-high-school plans. Many analyzed the influence of ability, as shown by either aptitude tests or high school records, and the influence of economic status, as shown by occupation of father, income, or student's description of the family's economic level. Some considered the cultural-social level of the student as shown by parent's education, number of books in the home, or interests and activities of the

15

family. Others analyzed the effect of where the student lived, comparing rural and urban students, suburban and metropolitan students, or students living at varying distances from colleges. A few studies took into consideration the size of the high school, and a few the personality characteristics, attitudes, and values of students and their families. Only one of the studies reviewed here considered the influence of race, comparing white and colored students.

When the studies are considered together and one examines the relationships found between the variables studied and college attendance, one is immediately impressed by the almost completely positive results reported. Each of the studies that compared the sexes found differences. Each of the studies that examined ability and post-high-school plans found relationships. Every study but one — and that one confined to a very homogeneous sample — that analyzed economic status and plans found a relationship. Each study on the influence of cultural level found a difference. All but one of the studies on the influence of where the student lived found a relationship. Consistently the studies found a relationship between size of the high school and post-high-school plans, and almost as consistently, between plans and personality variables. Apparently investigators either have excluded in their studies variables not related to post-high-school plans or they have failed to report negative results.

The almost complete agreement found for these relationships regardless of variables examined is not surprising when one considers that the variables themselves are highly intercorrelated. The sex variable is perhaps the only one not having at least a moderate relationship with other indices. Ability, economic level, cultural level, and area from which the student comes all seem to be related. Children of men in professions tend to obtain higher ability scores than children of men in unskilled jobs. Men in higher economic levels tend to be better educated. Urban-rural differences are related to income, education, and financial status. High school size is related to area. Some evidence suggests that even tenuous personality variables are related to area and certainly to social and cultural level. Simple, first-order relationships between these variables and the plans of students all tend to be in the same direction.

A few studies have attempted to analyze interactions; for example, when one holds ability constant, how does this affect the relationship

16

between economic status and post-high-school plans? In general, when such analyses have been made, the size of the observed relationships tends to diminish, but the significance remains: when in these studies one compares on the basis of ability and family's economic status students planning on college and those planning otherwise, large and significant differences emerge. When one takes groups of students planning to attend college and planning otherwise, but matched on the basis of economic status, one still finds a relationship between ability and plans, although it tends to be different from the relationship observed for the total group disregarding economic status.

The 1950 study of Minnesota students used information from a questionnaire entitled "After High School — What?" and test scores obtained from about 25,000 (over 90 per cent) high school seniors in public and private schools. About one third of these students were planning to attend college. Substantially more boys than girls so planned, and the proportion of students planning on college was much greater among urban than among farm children. A marked relationship was found between plans and college aptitude as indicated both by tests and high school grades, and substantial relationships were found between plans and family economic status and between plans and family cultural status. When interactions between sex and ability, area and sex, and the other variables were analyzed as related to post-high-school plans, the general picture emerged that a student's plans were simply one part of a complex and elaborate network of psychological and social variables.

"The forces influencing the decisions of the 25,000 boys and girls we studied are complex and present a puzzle of causal relationships. . . . The desire to attend college is closely related to our class structure. This class structure, in turn, can be conceptualized successfully in terms of economic status and cultural status. This conceptualization helps explain in part why some high school seniors plan to attend college and why others make alternative plans" (Berdie, 1954, p. 86).

Of 1053 Cleveland, Ohio, high school seniors studied in 1950, 50 per cent intended to attend college. Post-high-school plans were found to be related to sex, ability, and family economic level (White, 1952).

The plans of 1742 above-average high school seniors in New Mexico in 1952–53, and plans of another group of 1079 high school seniors from the upper 25 per cent of the class in 1954, were studied by using

17

both interviews and records. In the first group, about 62 per cent planned to attend college and approximately 55 per cent actually did so. In the second group approximately 59 per cent attended college. One or both of these studies identified relationships between plans and sex, economic status, cultural status, and region in which the student lived (Smith, Mathany, and Milfs, 1960).

In 1955, of 3479 high school graduates in the upper 10 per cent of Indiana high school classes, 65 per cent went to college, with college attendance being related to sex and economic status (Beezer and Hjelm, 1961).

Studies in Kansas from 1955 to 1957 revealed that 40 per cent of high school seniors attended college, with 65 per cent of the top third doing so. College attendance was related to sex, economic status, region in which the student lived, and size of high school (Beezer and Hjelm, 1961).

A series of reports are available from Kentucky extending from 1956 through 1960. The state Department of Education reported that between 1956 and 1959 from 31 to 35 per cent of Kentucky high school graduates attended college (Beezer and Hjelm, 1961). In 1959 Youmans reported that in 480 rural low-income families about 25 per cent of the children planned to attend college, and these plans were related to ability and attitudes. McDaniel and Forenback in 1960 reported that of 3178 Kentucky students (in the top 15 per cent of the high school class), 76 per cent attended college; attendance was related to sex and ability, but not to the area in which the student lived.

A comprehensive study in 1957 of Arkansas high school seniors showed that of 12,746 seniors who responded to questionnaires, 45 per cent planned to attend college, but letters to principals later revealed that only 26 per cent actually did so. Plans and attendance were related to sex, color, ability, economic level, cultural level, area in which the student lived, and size of high school. In this same group, of the top one third, 56 per cent actually attended college; of the top one fourth, 47 per cent (Stroup and Andrew, 1959).

Another comprehensive study, of Wisconsin high school graduates of 1957, was reported by Little (1959). A random one-sixth sample consisting of 5679 seniors was studied with questionnaires completed by both students and parents. Of these students, 30 per cent planned on college and 29 per cent actually attended. Plans were related to sex, intelligence, economic level, and perhaps, although less definitely, to attitudes or personality. In this group the top 15 per cent were studied separately, and here 65 per cent were planning to attend college, again with the same variables, for the most part, related to plans.

Two studies have been reported of Chicago, Illinois, high school graduates of 1960 and 1961. January graduates of 1961 numbered 6251, June graduates of 1960 numbered 12,653. In each of these groups 48 per cent planned to attend college (Anonymous, 1960).

Table 1. Percentage of Minnesota High School Graduates Attending College within One Year of Graduation for 1938, 1945, and 1950

Group	1938	1945	1950
Boys	24%	24%	36%
Girls	20	21	27
Boys and girls	23	23	32
Metropolitan	26	25	39
Nonmetropolitan	21		28

Generalizations from these state-wide or in-state studies are difficult: studies are seldom conducted in different states during the same years, the populations are seldom defined in the same way, and the same or even comparable methods are seldom used for eliciting data. The results reviewed here do suggest that the proportions of students of different kinds planning to attend college vary from state to state, from year to year, and that possibly different conditions are not consistent from state to state and from year to year within the same state. One could generalize and say that in every state studied there is a tendency for more bright students than dull students to attend college, for more wealthy students than poor students, for more men than women, and for more students from homes with high than from homes with low parental education. In general, where a student lives within a state seems to have some influence.

Minnesota Studies. A summary prepared by Corcoran and Keller (1957) reveals for at least one state changes in proportions of high school graduates attending college within one year of graduation for three separated periods of time. The percentages of Minnesota high

19

school graduates in 1938, 1945, and 1950 who attended college are shown in Table 1.

Studies of Minnesota students during the past decade allow inferences to be made concerning differences within a state. In 1953 Nelson and McFarland (1962) studied the plans of 396 rural high school graduates. Twenty-three per cent were planning to attend college. Of the upper half of the class, somewhat fewer than 50 per cent were planning to attend college. In 1955 a report was distributed by the Guidance Office for the St. Cloud Technical High School. Of 225 graduates, 164 completed questionnaires showing 30 per cent of them attended college. In 1958 Johnson (1959) reported that of 657 Minneapolis high school graduates in the upper 17 per cent of their class, 81 per cent attended college. There was a marked sex difference. In 1960 Hagenah studied the educational plans of 703 Minnesota honors graduates as these plans were reported in a newspaper story and found that 78 per cent planned to attend college. In 1960 the Student Counseling Bureau of the University of Minnesota studied the plans of 47,394 high school juniors and found that 40 per cent planned to attend college, with a marked relationship between the plans of these students and their scores on college aptitude tests.

Nationwide Studies. Because of the differences among states and years, as well as the differences resulting from varying methods, estimates for the entire United States are difficult to make. In 1954 Wolfle estimated that 35 per cent of high school graduates in the United States entered college, with approximately 21 per cent eventually graduating from college. Of the total age group at that time, about 57.5 per cent graduated from high school, 20 per cent entered college, and almost 12 per cent graduated from college.

Cole, in 1955, reported on a 5 per cent national sample of public high school seniors, consisting of 33,000 students who provided information on a questionnaire. Of these students, 45 per cent planned on college and these plans were related to sex, ability, economic and cultural status, and area in which the student lived. Of students roughly in the top 30 per cent of this sample, about 63 per cent planned on college and approximately 54 per cent actually attended college shortly after graduating from high school. Again, for this high-ability group, sex, intelligence, economic, and cultural differences were found.

20

In 1955 Flynt estimated that approximately 50 per cent of all high school graduates in the top fourth of their class attended college. He also reported that about 60,000 persons of equal ability never did graduate from high school. Bridgman reported in 1959 that 46 per cent of recent high school graduates may have attended college at some time and that of the upper 30 per cent in graduating classes, 69 out of 100 attended college. Within the upper tenth, three out of four students attended college.

A study in 1959 of a probability sample of United States parents revealed that 49 per cent had plans for their children to attend college, these plans being related to economic and cultural level of the home and color of the student (Lansing, Lorimer, and Moriguchi, 1960). Using an extremely selected sample in 1957, Thistlethwaite (1958) reported that of 15,000 near-winners in the National Merit Scholarship competition, perhaps the upper 6 per cent of the high school population, 96 per cent attended college, with attendance related to sex, ability, and cultural level of the home.

The Bureau of Labor Statistics (1962) reported that 48 per cent of high school graduates in 1961 attended college, with 45 per cent being full-time college students. College attendance was related to sex.

Estimates of talent loss among high-ability students, as presented in Table 2, obviously depend on how the population was defined and when the study was made. The talent loss in 1953 among the highest 31 per cent of high school graduates amounted to 53 per cent. Four years later the talent loss of merit scholars, perhaps in the upper 1 per cent, amounted to 0.2 per cent. The figures suggest that although the talent loss is not large proportionately, the thousands of high-ability high school graduates who fail to attend college should be a cause of distress to all who are eager to increase the number of well-educated persons in the country.

A report by Walker (1962) provides interesting information on changes over time in the educational level of the country. Almost half of 4300 young men surveyed in 1960 had more schooling than their fathers had, 40 per cent had as much schooling, and only one out of ten had less than his father. About 68 per cent graduated from high school, as compared with about 33 per cent of their fathers. Of every one hundred young men with fathers who did not graduate from high school, over 15 per cent graduated from college. For every one hundred young

21

Table 2. Estimates of Talent Loss among Students of High Ability *

Source	Population	Date of Graduation from High School	Estimated Percentage Not Going to College
National Merit Scholarship Program	Merit Scholars (N = 827) 1957	1957	0.2†
	Finalists (N = 6,428) 1957	1957	3.1
	Semifinalists (N = 7,690) 1957	1957	5.1
	Total (N = 14,945) 1957	1957	3.9
Terman and Oden (1957)	Highest 1 or 2 per cent by IQ in California schools 1928	1928	12
Phearman (1949)	Highest 2 per cent by achievement tests among Iowa high school graduates 1947	1947	8
Wolfle (1954)	Highest 2.8 per cent of high school graduates on intelligence test 1953	1953	39
Phearman (1949)	Highest 9 per cent of Iowa's high school graduates 1947	1947	36
Iffert (1956)	Highest 10 per cent in high school graduating class 1950	1950	28
Corcoran and Keller (1957)	Highest 15 per cent by IQ of Minnesota high school seniors 1950	1950	33‡
Wolfle (1954)	Highest 8.8 per cent of high school graduates 1953	1953	45
Educational Testing Service (1957)	Highest 10 per cent by aptitude test of public high school seniors 1955	1955	30
Iffert (1956)	Highest 30 per cent in high school graduating class 1950	1950	30
Wolfle (1954)	Highest 31 per cent of high school graduates 1953	1953	53
Educational Testing Service (1957)	Highest scoring 30 per cent of public high school seniors 1955	1955	47

* Reprinted with permission from *Science*, Vol. 128, No. 3328 (October 10, 1958), p. 826, "The Conservation of Intellectual Talent," by Donald L. Thistlethwaite.

† Two students awarded scholarships are having their scholarships held for one year.

‡ Percentage attending college within four years of graduation.

men whose fathers graduated from high school but did not attend college, more than a third graduated from college. Of the young men whose fathers are college graduates, 80 per cent were expected to graduate from college. (See the chart on page 23 for a graphic comparison.)

RÉSUMÉ

Although much of our information is incomplete, it does allow us to make some generalizations concerning post-high-school plans, particu-

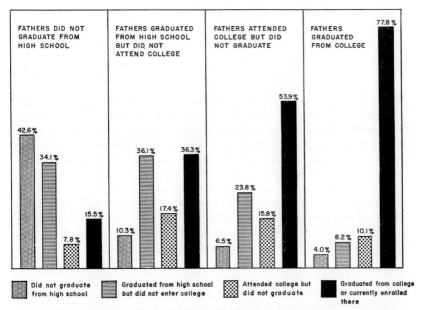

Educational status of young men from 20 to 24 years old, grouped by the educational attainment of their fathers, October 1960 (from *School Life*, April 1962)

larly as they involve college attendance. Many social and psychological variables enter into the picture. These plans and their determinants vary from state to state and no one state can be considered typical of the entire country.

The proportion of high school graduates attending college is steadily increasing. More men than women attend college; college attendance is related to economic and occupational status, as well as to cultural and educational status; and where a student lives within a state makes a difference, particularly in relation to the location of colleges.

These many variables not only set limits and provide opportunities which directly affect the decisions of students; they also affect attitudes and expectations, and these values are the implements or the means through which social conditions determine the decisions and choices of students. For any given student a single variable may determine his decision. A student whose family strongly opposes college may fail to attend college in spite of all other conditions. For no single group of students will any primary variable be isolated, and in any group one

23

can expect to find a complex of conditions related to post-high-school decisions. When all variables point in a particular direction, there is no question what the student will do upon graduation. When they point in different directions, the student has a difficult time making this very important decision. This process is very aptly described by Tyler (1959):

With the swift passage of the years one becomes acutely aware that the human life is finite. It lasts only a limited time, and each person has only a limited number of hours each day at his disposal. Only a small fraction of these potentialities with which his life begins can ever become realities. By the time his infancy is over, a considerable number of them have already been ruled out by the fact that he has spent his most formative years in one particular kind of home rather than another. But the person is still confronted at each step of his life with an incredibly complex assortment of stimulating conditions and behavior possibilities. In order to function at all, each of us must choose from this plethora of possibilities and organize what he has chosen.

REFERENCES

Anonymous. "State-Wide Testing Tops 16,000 for New Record." *The Kentucky Cooperative Newsletter*, 1–4. 1960.
———. *Summary of Immediate Plans of Chicago Public High School Graduates.* Chicago: Bureau of Pupil Personnel Services, 1960–1961.
American Council on Education. "Expectations for College High, Planning Inadequate According to New Study." *Higher Education and National Affairs* (American Council on Education), 8 (1959), 6–8.
Beezer, R. H., and H. F. Hjelm. *Factors Related to College Attendance.* Washington: U.S. Department of Health, Education, and Welfare, Office of Education, 1961. OE-54023 Cooperative Research Monograph No. 8.
Berdie, R. F. *After High School — What?* Minneapolis: University of Minnesota Press, 1954.
———. "Skilled Manpower from the High Schools." *School and Society*, 86 (1958), 8–9.
Bridgman, D. S. *Losses of Intellectual Talent from the Educational System Prior to Graduation from College.* Washington: National Science Foundation, 1959.
———. "Where the Loss of Talent Occurs and Why," in *College Admissions 7: The Search for Talent.* New York: College Entrance Examination Board, 1960.
Bureau of Labor Statistics. *School Life*, 44 (July 1962), No. 9, 37.
Cole, C. C., Jr. "Current Loss of Talent from High School to College: Summary of a Report." *Higher Education*, 12 (1955), 35–38.
———. *Encouraging Scientific Talent.* New York: College Entrance Examination Board, 1956.
Corcoran, Mary, and R. J. Keller. *College Attendance of Minnesota High School Seniors.* Minneapolis: University of Minnesota Bureau of Institutional Research, 1957.
Cowen, P. A. *Factors Related to the College Plans of High School Seniors.* Albany: University of the State of New York Division of Research in Higher Education, 1960.

Cowhig, J., J. Artis, J. A. Beegle, and H. Goldsmith. *Orientations toward Occupation and Residence.* Ann Arbor: Michigan State University Agricultural Experiment Station, 1960.

Educational Testing Service. "Factors Affecting Attendance at College Are Same Factors Affecting College Plans." *E.T.S. Developments,* 5 (1957), No. 3, p. 1.

Ellis, B. W. "Why Not College?" *California Guidance Newsletter,* 17 (1963), 3–4.

Flanagan, J. C., J. T. Dailey, M. F. Shaycoft, D. B. Orr, and I. Goldberg. *Studies of the American High School.* Project Talent Monograph Series, No. 2. Pittsburgh, Pa.: University of Pittsburgh, 1962.

Flynt, R. C. M. "America's Resources of Undeveloped Talent." *School Life,* 37 (1955), 122–124.

Foster, Emery. "School Retention Rate Rises." *School Life,* 42 (1960), 20–21.

Grant, W. V. "Employment of High School Graduates." *School Life,* 44 (1962), 37.

Hagenah, Theda. *Post-High-School Plans of 703 Honors Graduates.* Minneapolis: University of Minnesota Student Counseling Bureau, 1960. (Mimeographed.)

Jamrich, J. X. News release in *American Association of Land Grant College and State Universities Circular Letter,* 6 (1960).

Lansing, J. B., T. Lorimer, and C. Moriguchi. *How People Pay for College.* Ann Arbor: University of Michigan Survey Research Center, 1960.

Little, J. K. *Explorations into the College Plans and Experiences of High School Graduates.* Madison: University of Wisconsin School of Education, 1959.

———. "The Wisconsin Study of High School Graduates." *Educational Record,* 40 (1959), 123–128.

McDaniel, E. D., and M. S. Forenback. *Kentucky's Top Fifteen Percent: A Study of the College Attendance Patterns of Superior High School Students.* Lexington: University of Kentucky, Kentucky Cooperative Counseling and Testing Service, 1960.

Johnson, R. H. *Follow-Up Study: 1958 Graduates.* Minneapolis: Minneapolis Public School Division of Secondary Education Department of Counseling, 1959. (Mimeographed.)

National Science Foundation. *The Duration of Formal Education for High-Ability Youth.* Washington: National Science Foundation, n.d.

Nelson, T. M., and K. N. McFarland. "Occupational Patterns of Rural Youth." *Vocational Guidance Quarterly,* 10 (1962), 164–166.

Schoening, L. H., E. W. Hughes, and Alice Jacobsen. *Ten Year Follow-Up Study of Winona Senior High School Graduates.* Winona, Minn.: Guidance Department, Winona Public Schools, 1955.

Smith, S. E., H. V. Mathany, and M. M. Milfs. *Are Scholarships the Answer?* Albuquerque: University of New Mexico Press, 1960.

Sorenson, R. H., and R. C. Miller. *Report on Follow-Up Survey of Technical School Graduates (Class of 1955). Two Years after Graduation.* St. Cloud, Minn.: Technical High School, 1957.

Stroup, Francis, and D. C. Andrew. *Barriers to College Attendance.* Magnolia, Ark.: Southwest, 1959.

Thistlethwaite, D. L. "The Conservation of Intellectual Talent." *Science,* 128 (1958), 822–826.

———. *Recruitment and Retention of Talented College Students.* Nashville, Tenn.: Vanderbilt University, 1963.

Tyler, Leona E. "Toward a Workable Psychology of Individuality." *American Psychologist,* 14 (1959). Reprinted in M. T. Mednick, and S. A. Mednick, *Research in Personality* (New York: Holt, Rinehart, and Winston, 1963).

Walker, R. M. "Educational Level of Young Men Today Compared with That of Their Fathers." *School Life,* 44 (1962), 18.

White, R. C. *These Will Go to College.* Cleveland, Ohio: The Press of Western Reserve University, 1952.

Wolfle, Dael. *America's Resources of Specialized Talent.* New York: Harper and Brothers, 1954.

Youmans, E. G. "Backgrounds of Rural Youth Planning to Enter College." *Journal of Educational Sociology*, 32 (1959), 152–156.

· **2**

An Overview: Results and Implications

A SURVEY of all graduating seniors in Minnesota high schools was undertaken in 1950 to identify their post-high-school plans and the conditions related to these plans. The survey revealed how many of the total number of students and how many from a sample of high-ability students planned to attend college, to enter nurses' training, to obtain other types of post-high-school training, and to seek employment. These plans were related to tested academic ability, high school achievement, family economic and cultural status, and other social and psychological variables. A follow-up study one year after these students graduated revealed the extent to which plans stated during the senior year were indicative of later actual behavior, and a further follow-up study in 1954 provided additional information. Studies conducted in other states since 1950 have been modeled after the Minnesota study and have confirmed its results. A study in 1961 consisted of a repetition and an extension of the 1950 Minnesota study so that conditions existing at these two times could be compared. In this way, changes and trends occurring during this eleven-year period could be determined and analyzed. During these years the proportion of students planning to attend college and the influences determining these plans have changed. The results of this research provide a perspective to aid in understanding current conditions and reveal information useful in planning.

Since 1950 several developments have occurred in Minnesota's educational system and in the nation as a whole. The number of high school counselors has increased many times. The training and competency of counselors have improved as a result of better undergraduate and graduate training programs. The profession of high school counseling has

27

been more clearly defined; more school facilities and personnel are available; counseling and guidance methods have improved; and the counseling provisions of the National Defense Education Act have stimulated over-all development. National programs have been established to identify talented young people and encourage them to continue their training. The country's population and resources have grown. The existence of large numbers of unskilled workers facing unemployment while shortages occurred in many fields requiring specialized skills has emphasized the importance of higher levels of training. Higher education has received much attention, particularly since the accomplishments of Russian scientists have become known in the United States. Parents, teachers, and others in the community have been made increasingly aware of the importance of the utilization of manpower resources.

MAJOR OBJECTIVES OF THE 1961 SURVEY

The survey and analysis in 1961 were directed at the following questions: (1) What changes occurred between 1950 and 1961 in the proportions of high school seniors planning to attend a college or university, enter nursing, seek other types of training, enter military service, and seek employment? (2) To what extent did proportions of high-ability students making these plans change between 1950 and 1961 and what have been the relationships between ability and these plans? (3) What are the relationships of socioeconomic, cultural, and family conditions to students' post-high-school plans, and how have these relationships changed over the eleven-year period? (4) What are the relationships between personal attitudes and values and the post-high-school plans of seniors? (5) What are the relationships between changes in proportions of students with varying plans and changes in their schools, guidance programs, and communities over this eleven-year period?

PROCEDURES IN THE 1961 SURVEY

The Questionnaire. To gather information about students, a questionnaire entitled "After High School — What?" was developed which resembled the one used in 1950, with some modifications. (See pages 29–32.) The most significant change was the addition of twenty-five items at the end of the questionnaire to elicit information regarding attitudes and values.

28

UNIVERSITY OF MINNESOTA

OFFICE OF THE DEAN OF STUDENTS

STUDENT COUNSELING BUREAU

H.S. _____1-3

Iden. No._____4-6

After High School—What?

For High School Seniors

1961

In order to provide information about what high school seniors are planning for the next year and to show the reasons for these plans, you are being asked to answer the questions below.

Write in the answer or place a check mark (√) before the appropriate word or phrase.

7-20. Name (Print)_____

                  Last   First   Middle

21. (1)_____Male (2) _____Female

22-23. Age last birthday_____ years

24. Occupation of father: (Check the item which applies)

(1)_____Profession (lawyer, banker, doctor, teacher, minister, dentist, etc.)

(2)_____Owns or manages business (store, gas station or garage, photography or barber shop, insurance agency, hotel or cafe, repair shop, newspaper, etc.)

(3)_____Office work (bookkeeper, cashier, postal clerk, etc.)

(4)_____Sales (insurance, real estate, retail store, etc.)

(5)_____Owns or manages farm

(6)_____Skilled tradesman (carpenter, electrician, machinist)

(7)_____Factory worker (laborer, farm laborer, janitor, mine laborer)

(   ) Other occupations: (Be specific)

_____
(Write in name of occupation)

25. Education of father: (Check highest level attained)

(1)_____Did not attend school

(2)_____Some grade school

(3)_____Completed eighth grade

(4)_____Some high school

(5)_____Graduated from high school

(6)_____Business or trade school

(7)_____Some college work (including teacher training)

(8)_____Graduated from college

(9)_____Holds more than one college degree

26. Education of mother: (Check highest level attained)

(1)_____Did not attend school

(2)_____Some grade school

(3)_____Completed eighth grade

(4)_____Some high school

(5)_____Graduated from high school

(6)_____Business or trade school

(7)_____Some college work (including teacher training)

(8)_____Graduated from college

(9)_____Holds more than one college degree

27. Which of the following ways best describes how your family gets its income? (Check the one phrase which best applies)

(1)_____Professional fees or business profits (Including profits from farms)

(2)_____Fixed salary (Paid on a monthly or yearly basis)

(3)_____Wages (Paid on an hourly or daily basis and depending on number of hours worked)

(4)_____Income from investments (Stocks, bonds, real estate, insurance)

(5)_____Pensions (Government or other)

28. Check the phrase which best describes your family's income:

(1)_____Frequently have difficulty making ends meet

(2)_____Sometimes have difficulty in getting the necessities

(3)_____Have all the necessities but not many luxuries

(4)_____Comfortable but not well-to-do

(5)_____Well-to-do

(6)_____Wealthy

29. Course or curriculum taken in high school: (Check the one which best describes your course)

(1)_____Commercial (2)_____Agriculture (3)_____Shop or Technical (4)_____College Preparatory (5)_____General

(   ) Other_____
(Write in)

30-31. Check the most important reason or reasons why you originally selected the course you checked in item 29:

30
(1)_____ Only one offered in school
(2)_____ Teacher's advice
(3)_____ Counselor's advice
(4)_____ Parent's advice
(5)_____ Required to by school
(6)_____ Brothers or sisters took it
(7)_____ Seemed easiest
(8)_____ Required by parents

31
(1)_____ Was best in this work
(2)_____ Fitted vocational plans best
(3)_____ Course seemed most interesting
(4)_____ Friends took it
(5)_____ Brother's or sister's advice
(6)_____ "Everyone else" took it
(7)_____ Don't know
(   ) Other_____
(Write in)

32-33-34. What are your plans for next year (1961-1962)? (Check the **one** plan you are now most seriously considering)

32
(1)_____ Get a job.. If yes, what kind of work?_____
(2)_____ Work for parents... If yes, what kind of work?_____
(3)_____ Go to college... If. yes, which college?_____
(4)_____ Go to trade school....................................... If yes, which school?_____
(5)_____ Go to business school.................................... If yes, which school?_____
(6)_____ Go to other school....................................... If yes, which school?_____
(7)_____ Do postgraduate work in high school
(8)_____ Enter the Military Service
(9)_____ Other_____
(Write in)

33-34

35-36. Check the reasons for making the plans you indicated above:

35
(1)_____ To prepare for a vocation
(2)_____ To be with old school friends
(3)_____ To get a liberal education
(4)_____ To start making money quickly
(5)_____ To please parents or friends
(6)_____ To be independent
(7)_____ To make friends and helpful connections

36
(1)_____ It is "the thing to do"
(2)_____ Foregone conclusion, never questioned why
(3)_____ Will enable me to make more money
(4)_____ "Everyone here" does this
(5)_____ Tired of studying, have had enough education
(6)_____ Only thing I can afford to do
(7)_____ Like school
(8)_____ Other_____
(Explain)

37. Has marriage or the early prospect of marriage influenced your plans for the coming year?
(1)_____ Yes (2)_____ No

38. In your present thinking, have you any idea when you plan to get married?
(1)_____ Already married
(2)_____ This year
(3)_____ Next year
(4)_____ In a few years
(5)_____ Can't say
(6)_____ Not planning on marriage

39. If you are going to college next year (1961-1962), to what extent will your family help you pay expenses?
(1)_____ Pay all my expenses
(2)_____ Pay most of my expenses
(3)_____ Pay some of my expenses
(4)_____ Pay none of my expenses

40. If you are not going to college, would you change your plans and attend college if you had more money?
(1)_____ Yes (0)_____ No

41. If you checked "Yes" to the last item, how much more money would you need to attend college?
(1)_____ Enough to pay all my expenses
(2)_____ Enough to pay about half my expenses
(3)_____ Enough to pay less than half my expenses

42. If you are not going to college, could you afford to go if you wished to go?
(1)_____ Could afford it easily
(2)_____ Could barely afford it
(3)_____ Could afford it but it would involve many sacrifices
(4)_____ Could not afford it

43. How does your family feel about your going to college?
(1)_____Insists that I go   (3)_____Is indifferent
(2)_____Wants me to go   (4)_____Doesn't want me to go
                                      (5)_____Won't allow me to go

44. If you are planning on college, are you considering any graduate or professional training after your undergraduate college work?
(1)_____Yes (0)_____No   If "Yes," indicate type_____

45. If you are **not** going to college next year, do you plan to go at some later date?
(x)_____No
_____Yes (If you checked "yes" here, indicate when you plan to attend college):
(1)_____After 1 year   (2)_____After 2 years   (3)_____After 3 years   (4)_____After 4 or more years

46. Do you have a furnace or central heating in your home?   53. Do you have a television set in your home?
(1)_____Yes (0)_____No   (1)_____Yes (0)_____No

47. Do you have running water in your home?   54. Does your family own your home?
(1)_____Yes (0)_____No   (1)_____Yes (0)_____No

48. Do you have both hot and cold running water?   55. How many people live in your home?_____(   )
(1)_____Yes (0)_____No

49. Do you have an electric or gas refrigerator?   56. How many rooms are there in your home
(1)_____Yes (0)_____No   excluding the bath room?_____(   )

50. Do you have a telephone in your home?   57. How many people excluding yourself sleep in
(1)_____Yes (0)_____No   your room? _____(,

51. Does your family own or rent a deep freeze unit or a locker? 58. How many passenger cars does your family own? (Check)
(1)_____Yes (0)_____No   0_____   1_____   2 or more_____

52. Do you have electric lights in your home?   59. What is the year and make of your family's newest car?
(1) _____Yes (0)_____No   Year_____ Make_____ (   ) (   )
          (Items 53-59 in next column)

60. Do you live on a farm? (1)_____Yes (0)_____No

61. If you live on a farm, have you had a major responsibility for a part of its management?
(1)_____Yes (0)_____No

62. If you live on a farm, is there a place for you in its operation which would provide a good future for you if you should wish to stay?
(1)_____Yes (0)_____No

63. Approximately how many books does your family have in your home? (Check appropriate category)
(1)_____ 0- 9   (3)_____25-49   (5)_____100-up
(2)_____10-24   (4)_____50-99

64-65-66. Which of these magazines does your family subscribe to or regularly buy?

64	65	66
(1)_____Reader's Digest	(1)_____Redbook	(1)_____U. S. News & World Report
(2)_____Life	(2)_____National Geographic Magazine	(2)_____Sports Afield
(3)_____Saturday Evening Post	(3)_____Time	(3)_____Sports Illustrated
(4)_____Look	(4)_____True	(4)_____Holiday
(5)_____McCall's Magazine	(5)_____Parents' Magazine	(5)_____New Yorker
(6)_____Ladies Home Journal	(6)_____Capper's Farmer	(6)_____Fortune
(7)_____Better Homes and Gardens	(7)_____Argosy	(7)_____The Farmer
(8)_____Good Housekeeping	(8)_____Popular Mechanics	(8)_____Atlantic Monthly
(9)_____American Home	(9)_____Popular Science	(9)_____Harper's
(0)_____Coronet	(0)_____Newsweek	
(x)_____Farm Journal	(x)_____Successful Farming	

67. Others_____

68-69-70. To which of these organizations does your father or mother or both belong?

68
(1)_____P.T.A. or Mothers' Club
(2)_____American Legion or VFW
(3)_____Rotary
(4)_____Knights of Columbus
(5)_____Elks
(6)_____Masons
(7)_____Eastern Star
(8)_____Odd Fellows
(9)_____Rebeccas
(0)_____Lions

69
(1)_____Moose
(2)_____Eagles
(3)_____Labor Union
(4)_____Farm Bureau
(5)_____Farm Union
(6)_____Grange

69 (Cont.)
(7)_____Chamber of Commerce or Community Business Club
(8)_____Kiwanis
(9)_____Shrine
(0)_____Ladies' Aid

70
(1)_____League of Womens Voters
(2)_____Neighborhood or other social card playing group
(3)_____Country club or golf club
(4)_____Study or literary club
(5)_____American Automobile Association (AAA)
(6)_____A sportsman club
(7)_____American Association of University Women
(8)_____National origin group (such as Sons of Norway)
(9)_____Church club or group
(0)_____Athletic club or group
(x)_____Hobby club or group
(   ) Others_____

The following items are related to your attitudes, feelings, and experiences. Remember that all of the information on this questionnaire is treated as confidential. Circle T if the item is true for you and F if it is false.

21. T F I meet strangers easily.

22. T F I get along as well as the average person in social activities.

23. T F In school I sometimes have been sent to the principal for cutting up.

24. T F I feel self-conscious when reciting in class.

25. T F I am sure I get a raw deal from life.

26. T F I feel at ease with people.

27. T F At times I have very much wanted to leave home.

28. T F I have difficulty in starting a conversation with a person who has just been introduced.

29. T F I find it hard to keep my mind on a task or job.

30. T F I enjoy speaking before groups of people.

31. T F I know who is responsible for most of my troubles.

32. T F My parents have often objected to the kind of people I go around with.

33. T F I am rather shy in contacts with people.

34. T F No one seems to understand me.

35. T F I enjoy entertaining people.

36. T F My family does not like the work I have chosen or the work I intend to choose for my life work.

37. T F I like to meet new people.

38. T F My parents and family find more fault with me than they should.

39. T F I dislike social affairs.

40. T F If people had not had it in for me I would have been much more successful.

41. T F I find it easy to express my ideas.

42. T F I wish I were not so shy.

43. T F I avoid people when it is possible.

44. T F I have had very peculiar and strange experiences.

45. T F I stay in the background at parties or social gatherings.

46. T F Most of my close friends are planning to go to college.

47. Would you say that your high school grades are a fairly accurate reflection of your ability?

1_____Yes 2_____No

48. Do you think that most of the important things that happen to people are: (Check one)

(1)_____More the result of circumstances beyond their control.

(2)_____More the result of their own efforts.

49. If you had your choice, which type of job would you pick? (Check one)

(1)_____A job which pays quite a low income but which you are sure of keeping.

(2)_____A job which pays a good income but which you have a 50-50 chance of losing.

(3)_____A job which pays an extremely good income if you make the grade but in which you lose almost everything if you don't make it.

(224-4)

Items retained from the 1950 questionnaire were left unchanged. In the earlier study comparisons were made between information provided by students on the questionnaire and information obtained from parents in interviews, which indicated that the students' responses on the questionnaire were reliable. Therefore, in 1961, parents were not interviewed, on the assumption that the data provided by the questionnaire would be likewise reliable.

Test Scores. For most students, a college aptitude test score was available. The Minnesota Scholastic Aptitude Test (MSAT), administered during the winter of the junior year in high school, provided a single score predictive of success in Minnesota colleges. The test is a shortened, time-limited form of the Ohio Psychological Examination, Form 26, developed by Professors W. L. Layton and H. A. Toops (Berdie, Layton, Swanson, *et al.*, 1962).

For each student a high school percentile rank was available, based on all grades earned during his freshman, sophomore, and junior years, or sophomore and junior years, depending on whether he was in a three- or four-year high school. The rank showed the relative standing of the student in his class. A percentile rank of 100 placed him in the top 1 per cent, a percentile rank of 1 placed him in the lower 1 per cent; a percentile rank of 47 indicated that 47 per cent of the students obtained a grade point average equal to or less than his. The high school percentile rank was one of the best predictors of academic success in Minnesota colleges. Whereas the Minnesota Scholastic Aptitude Test tended to predict grades as well as would be indicated by a correlation coefficient of .45 to .55, the high school percentile rank provided a correlation coefficient of from .50 to .60. High school percentile rank and MSAT score combined predicted as well as would be indicated by a multiple correlation coefficient of between .55 and .65.

School and Community Information. Information about the status of the school and community in 1961 and about school status in 1950 was collected by means of a school questionnaire mailed to selected school principals after the cooperation of their superintendents had been obtained through a letter.

Sample of Students. Each of the 560 high schools in Minnesota was asked to have its graduating seniors complete the questionnaire in January and February of 1961. These schools included all public and private high schools in the state. The questionnaire was given to seniors in 551 high schools, or 98 per cent of all schools. The total number of students completing usable questionnaires was 44,756, or 97 per cent of all graduating seniors. For almost everyone completing the questionnaire, test scores were available, although some who had taken the test did not complete the questionnaire and a few who did complete it had not been tested in their junior year.

Sample of Schools and Communities Studied. A sample of the state's secondary schools was selected for studying the relationship between changes in the percentages of college-bound students and changes in school and community characteristics. Before the schools to be used in this special study could be selected, the data from the questionnaires were tabulated. Selection was based on the size of the graduating class and the changes from 1950 to 1961 in percentages of seniors planning to attend college. Schools first were divided into three groups according to size of senior class. The small-school group consisted of schools having 30 or fewer seniors, the medium-size schools had between 31 and 100 seniors, and the large-school group contained those with more than 100 graduating seniors.

Within each group, the 10 per cent of the schools showing the largest percentage increase in seniors planning to attend college and the 10 per cent showing the smallest increase (or largest decrease) in college-bound students were selected for study. Questionnaire returns after intensive follow-up were obtained from 13 of the 14 small schools showing increases in percentages, 13 of the 14 small schools showing decreases, 24 of the 25 medium-size schools showing increases, 23 of the 25 medium-size schools showing decreases, 10 of the 11 large schools showing increases, and 10 of the 11 large schools showing decreases. Returns were obtained from 93 per cent of the schools. Complete data were not available for each of the schools since some omitted answers to certain questions. Further information concerning these schools is included in Chapter 7.

Analysis of the Student Data. Since large differences in post-high-school plans occur among students from different types of communities and between the sexes, groups were analyzed according to sex and type of residence area. The first group consisted of all students who lived on farms. The second consisted of metropolitan students from schools in Minneapolis, St. Paul, Duluth, and suburbs of these cities. The last, the nonfarm group, consisted of all other students, namely those who lived in villages, towns, and small cities. Each of these three groups was separated into boys and girls.

The resulting six groups were further divided into subgroups according to post-high-school plan: students bound for college, students planning to seek jobs, students planning to attend trade or business school, and the like.

A separate analysis was done for high-ability students. All of the 7351 students who had MSAT scores of 45 or above were selected and analyzed as was the total group. These high-ability students — the top 17 per cent of the 1961 seniors — compare favorably with the upper 25 per cent of freshmen entering Minnesota colleges. One can assume that practically all of these students had more than sufficient ability to succeed in any Minnesota college. High-ability students whose fathers were in either skilled or unskilled trades were the subject of a special, closer analysis.

Follow-Up Study. In the spring of 1962, a year after graduation, a sample of seniors who had completed the questionnaire was selected from the total population to provide a random sample consisting of approximately 1000 students from metropolitan schools and 1000 from nonmetropolitan schools. The actual sample sizes were 1082 metropolitan and 1021 nonmetropolitan students. Addresses used in locating these students were those they had provided when juniors; of the total group addresses were not available for 173 because of illegible handwriting or failure to provide the information. This left a total sample of 1930.

Each student in the follow-up study was sent a letter requesting him to participate and return a postcard questionnaire on which he was asked to check his principal activity for the past year and indicate the type of work or name of school if he checked these categories. He also was asked a question regarding any changes of plans he might be contemplating for the following year and a question regarding his marital status. Four follow-up letters were mailed to the nonrespondents at two- to three-week intervals. Data on responses to the follow-up questionnaire are presented in Table 3.

Eighty-four per cent of the sample had replied soon after the fourth follow-up letter was mailed. The return from the metropolitan areas

35

was 87 per cent, significantly greater than the 82 per cent return from the nonmetropolitan areas. Perhaps this was because a greater proportion of the metropolitan students were attending the university and were therefore more likely to respond to a questionnaire on the letterhead of the university. After the mail return had been completed, nonrespondents in the Minneapolis and St. Paul areas were followed up by telephone. Nearly a third of these had left the area and could not be located, but information was obtained for the remaining two thirds. The information requested was simple enough to be obtainable over the phone from almost anyone in the student's household. The percentage of returns in this way was increased to 93 per cent for the metropolitan area. This included 100 per cent of all metropolitan students located.

Table 3. Responses to the 1962 Follow-Up Questionnaire

Item	Metropolitan Group (971 mailed)		Nonmetropolitan Group (959 mailed)		Total (1930 mailed)	
	No.	%	No.	%	No.	%
Returned by mail	841	87	783	82*	1,624	84
Returned by phone	59	6			59	3
Unlocatable	71	7	63	7	134	7
Nonrespondent			113	12	113	6
Total returned	900	93	783	82	1,683	87

*Difference between returns by mail — metropolitan (87 per cent) vs. nonmetropolitan (82 per cent) — significant beyond .01 level.

SUMMARY OF FINDINGS

In 1961, of all Minnesota high school graduates, 41 per cent planned to attend college the year after graduation. The follow-up study one year after graduation showed that the proportion actually attending college closely resembled the proportion originally stating such plans.

The proportion of high school graduates attending college had increased slowly over the eleven-year period with the average increase amounting to approximately one half of one percentage point per year. In 1950, 35 per cent of the seniors planned to attend college; in 1961, 41 per cent so planned.

Of the graduating seniors surveyed in 1950, 64 per cent reported one year later that they had followed their plans; in 1961, 67 per cent so reported. Fewer farm students than others followed their plans. Eighty-four per cent of the students planning to attend college reported one year later that they had done so. Only 20 per cent of the students who planned to attend business school reported having done so.

Of students included in the follow-up study, 48 per cent had planned to attend college; 44 per cent one year later had attended college. As seniors, 22 per cent planned to get a job; one year later, 30 per cent reported actually having obtained jobs.

The proportionate increase of high-ability students who planned to attend college was far greater from 1950 to 1961 than the increase for the total group of high school graduates. Of students in the upper 17 per cent in 1961, 81 per cent planned to attend college. Of a similar group in 1950, only 67 per cent planned to attend college. The able group with an increase of 14 percentage points, showed an increase in college attendance plans of almost three times that for the total group. Of the 1908 students providing the top 4.5 per cent of graduating seniors, in the top decile on both MSAT and high school percentile rank, 88 per cent planned on college, including 95 per cent of the boys and 83 per cent of the girls. Among the girls in this group, 89 per cent from metropolitan areas and only 72 per cent from the farm areas planned to attend college. Ninety-seven per cent of the metropolitan boys and 94 per cent of the farm boys in this selected group had college plans.

Post-high-school plans were closely related to ability, economic, and cultural status, sex, area in which students lived, family attitudes, and personal values and aptitudes. In each case, each of these relationships was in the expected direction, similar in 1961 to that for 1950. Degrees of relationship between post-high-school plans and the variables differed in 1961 from those of 1950, and some evidence suggested that for at least some groups college attendance was increasingly related to ability and high school achievement and decreasingly related to economic status.

Fewer noncollege-planning students in 1961 than in 1950 stated the need for financial assistance if they were to attend college, but in some groups the fewer students stating such a need estimated that they would require more assistance than did students in the earlier year.

Marriage has some influence on post-high-school plans, although immediate marriage is given relatively little consideration in the plans of boys and affects the plans of only a few girls.

The total number of high-ability graduates in Minnesota not planning to attend college in 1961 was about 1600. Of these, 32 per cent said they would attend college if they could afford it. The average student in this latter group said he would require about half the amount needed to cover college expenses. Assuming the cost of college to be $1400 a year, the total amount needed by this group each year approximated $350,000.

Although changes in school conditions were not directly related to increases or decreases in proportions of graduates planning on college, status of a school at the beginning of a decade was indicative of whether these proportions increased or decreased in the following eleven years.

The personal attitudes and values of students were related to the sex, home area, and the post-high-school plans of the student. In general the relationships between the attitudes and plans were similar for the different sex and area groups. On the average, students planning to attend college indicated a greater social need and more social competencies than students planning to seek jobs. They described themselves more often as having no difficulty with family, other students, and school authorities. The data provided a picture of a large group of students, regardless of plans, who saw themselves as socially competent, comfortable, and well behaved.

SOME IMPLICATIONS

The introductory comments in the first chapter, the information on social changes in Chapter 3, and the review of the findings of others presented in Chapter 4, considered together with the results of the Minnesota studies, lead to speculations significant for students, their families, schools and colleges, and other social agencies. The statements that follow are not conclusions derived from the data analyzed, but rather are suggestions and ideas that are limited by the geographical focus of the studies. Although the studies were made in Minnesota in 1950 and 1961, their implications have relevance for American higher and secondary education today.

As the loss of talent before high school graduation and between high school and college diminishes, with fewer dropouts in high school and more students going on to college, colleges must become increasingly concerned with their responsibility for the large loss incurred by dropouts among competent students after matriculation. The earlier study by Iffert (1958) shows that almost as many students drop out of college as complete it, and many local studies suggest that the number who drop out of college does not consist entirely of those who lack ability or are incapable of benefiting from higher education. College failure rates can be reduced if college faculties improve their admissions, placement, instructional, examination, and grading methods, and if they provide careful, professional, and individual attention to students.

The inevitability of college attendance for many high school graduates not intellectually or socially motivated for traditional college courses requires the development of new forms of post-high-school education and of new and unique college programs. To meet these needs, the diversity already characterizing American higher education must be increased and encouraged. Pressures to standardize higher education must be resisted as well as pressures to standardize elementary and secondary education.

While the loss of talent between high school and college has diminished during past decades, special efforts are required to reduce talent loss for easily identified subgroups — women, children from farms, and children of unskilled workers. Although the Minnesota studies did not identify students from other minority or underprivileged groups, special efforts are obviously needed for these students.

Although the relative proportion of students requiring scholarships may not increase, with the increasing costs of higher education and larger numbers of students from lower economic levels it may become necessary to provide larger scholarships to induce more talented high school students to attend college. Scholarships may have to be committed to students before their high school graduation in order to stimulate their motivation to attend college.

A student's attending college is the result not only of his own motivation but of his family's, and efforts to induce more competent students to attend college must be directed toward both the family and the child.

Finally, the average quality of college students does not decline as the absolute and relative number of students increases. The data in these studies, as do data found elsewhere, indicate that the nation's pool of competent persons continues to expand, and that enough high-ability students now fail to attend college so that the proportion of persons in college can be increased in the future without seriously lowering the intellectual status of the total consumer group in higher education.

REFERENCES

Berdie, R. F., W. L. Layton, E. O. Swanson, T. Hagenah, and J. C. Merwin. *Counseling and the Use of Tests.* Minneapolis: University of Minnesota Press, 1962.

Iffert, R. E. "Retention and Withdrawal of College Students." *U.S. Office of Education Bulletin,* No. 1 (1958).

National and Community Changes

THE choices and decisions of students as they leave high school are behaviors resulting from their preferences, abilities, interests, and inclinations. Obviously the family and the school directly influence these decisions, and we are accustomed to regarding this behavior within the social context of parents, brothers and sisters, teachers, counselors, and friends. The social settings in which these behaviors occur, however, are much broader than the school or the family and indeed extend far beyond the student's immediate community. The purpose of this chapter is to describe the changes that occurred in this broader social context between 1950 and 1961, the era covered by our research, and to allow the reader to study their implications for student decisions.

Although social change seldom directly influences student decisions, as the contexts in which these decisions occur change the decisions will vary. Social pressures, educational resources, occupational opportunities, financial means, and public attitudes influence decisions, and the importance of these influences should not be overlooked when one concentrates on the characteristics of the student and his family.

The United States underwent many changes between 1950 and 1961. With the addition of two large states, the very size of the country expanded. The population exploded. Educational competencies among the public improved; activities altered. The country's wealth grew, and new ways of using this wealth were developed.

In 1950 the population of the United States was 152 million, and by 1960 had increased by 18 per cent.[1] The age distribution of the popula-

[1] Most of the statistics included in this chapter were obtained from the *Fact Book on Higher Education* distributed by the Office of Statistical Information and Re-

tion also shifted; in 1960 proportionately many more persons were under fifteen or over sixty-five. In the earlier year, 14.7 per cent of Americans were between the ages of fifteen and twenty-four years whereas in 1960 this percentage was 13.6. On the other hand, 26.9 per cent were under fifteen years of age in 1950 as compared with 31 per cent in 1960. In 1950, 8.1 per cent were over sixty-five years of age; in 1960, 9.2 per cent. In 1950, 3,632,000 babies were born; in 1960, 4,258,000. There were more persons of high school and college age in 1960 than in 1950, but they formed a proportionately smaller group in the total population. Students were surrounded by, cooperating with, and competing with a far larger group of persons in 1960 than they were in 1950.

Education in the United States changed greatly during the decade. Although major qualitative changes can be identified, the directly quantifiable developments should be of immediate concern. In 1950 the total enrollment in elementary and high schools was 25 million; in 1960, 36 million. The educational level of persons twenty-five years old or over showed dramatic changes. In 1950, 11 per cent of these adults had fewer than five years of education as compared with 8 per cent in 1960. In 1950, 48 per cent of adults had no more than an eighth-grade education, as compared with 39 per cent in 1960. In 1950, 52 per cent of adults had more than an eighth-grade education and 14 per cent had gone beyond high school. By 1960, 61 per cent of the population had more than an eighth-grade education and 16 per cent had more than twelve years of schooling.

Available figures suggest that these changes will continue in the same direction. In 1950, 44 per cent of persons between the ages of five and thirty-four years were in school as compared with 56 per cent in 1960. In the sixteen- to seventeen-year-old range, 71 per cent were in school in 1950, 77 per cent in 1960. In the eighteen- to nineteen-year-old range the figures were 29 and 32 per cent, and between the twenty- and twenty-four-year-old range 9 per cent were in school in 1950 and 11 per cent in 1960. In 1950, 1,199,700 persons graduated from high school; in 1960, 1,873,000. Whether or not Americans are being better educated, they are being more educated.

One of the most dramatic changes in American education is asso-

search, The American Council on Education, 1785 Massachusetts Ave. N.W., Washington 6, D.C.

ciated with higher education. In 1950, 26 out of every 100 persons between the ages of nineteen and twenty-one were in college. In 1960 this figure was 37 out of 100. Opening college enrollments totaled 2,296,000 in 1950, as compared with 3,610,000 in 1960. The number of students beginning college in 1950 was 516,000; in 1960, 929,000 — an increase of 80 per cent, four times greater than the increase one would expect on the basis of population growth.

During the decade from 1950 to 1960, educators — as well as many others — became increasingly concerned with the large loss of talent between high school and college. Nationwide talent search programs such as the National Merit Scholarship Program were instituted, and programs already in existence greatly increased their activity. Local testing programs within the schools and the number of counselors available to make use of them also increased dramatically. Able young people were therefore more likely to be identified, more likely to be encouraged to go to college. This increased support, both moral and financial, occurred not only within the school but also within the family and the larger community — and for girls as well as boys.

Although the number of college students increased dramatically, the increase in number of college degrees granted was comparatively moderate. In 1950, 456,000 degrees were granted; in 1960, 491,000. An interesting change did occur in that 27 per cent of these degrees were earned in 1950 by women, as compared with 34 per cent in 1960. The number of baccalaureate or first professional degrees granted varied according to specialty, as shown in the accompanying tabulation.

Specialty	1950	1960
Accounting	10,766	10,654
Agriculture	12,165	6,822
Business and commerce	58,237	57,309
Chemistry	8,258	7,604
Education	62,000	93,000
Engineering	41,893	35,860
Mathematics	5,753	13,127
Pharmacy	4,622	3,092
Psychology	7,189	8,524
Russian	28	195

The number of degrees given in some areas showed a significant decrease; most striking are the changes in pharmacy, agriculture, and engineering. The decline in the number of agriculture degrees is not surprising in view of the decreasing numbers of persons engaged in

43

agricultural occupations, and perhaps the decrease in pharmacy degrees is related to changing professional practices. The decrease in engineering degrees has surprised many, who understandably assumed that the great emphasis placed on the country's needs for more engineers would have the opposite effect. The figures in the tabulation pertain only to the first degree; when advanced, graduate, or second professional degrees are considered, a somewhat different picture emerges.

It should be pointed out, however, that much of the increased emphasis on the importance of higher education, particularly in scientific areas, did not occur until after 1957 when the achievements of Russian scientists became generally known. By 1960 it was still too early for many of the resulting influences on American schools and colleges to be reflected in statistics dealing with higher education.

Colleges and universities underwent many changes and grew considerably between 1950 and 1960. The number of persons on college faculties increased from 248,000 to 382,000 over the ten-year period. The percentage of gross national product spent on education increased from 3.5 to 5.0 per cent; the corresponding percentage spent for higher education alone increased from 1.0 to 1.3 per cent. One interesting change is suggested by the increase in the number of foreign students in American colleges, from 29,800 in 1950 to 53,000 in 1960. The total income of institutions of higher education increased from 2390 million dollars to 5813 million dollars in the period.

ECONOMIC CHANGES OVER THE DECADE

At the beginning of the fifties 152 million Americans were creating a gross national product (in today's dollars) of 285 billion dollars. By the end of the decade this gross national product exceeded 503 billion dollars. A better idea of the national income is provided when these dollars are equated to 1954 dollars. Then the 1950 product is 318 billion dollars, the 1960 product 440 billion. Some of the figures on the nation's economic status can be best understood when one remembers that the consumer's price index in 1950 was 90; in 1960 it was 110. The total public and private debt in 1950 was 490 billion dollars as compared with 883 billion in 1960. Of this, 21 billion in 1950 was for state and local indebtedness as compared with 60 billion in 1960. In 1950, 219 billion consisted of the federal debt as compared with 241 billion in 1960. The

44

private debt increased from 251 billion dollars in 1950 to 582 billion dollars in 1960. Although the total public and private debt almost doubled, the state and local debt almost tripled, the private debt almost doubled, and the federal debt increased by only 10 per cent. If indebtedness is considered a result of waste, the federal government was much more careful than its component units or its individual citizens. If debt is considered evidence of willingness to invest in the future, the federal government may be doing relatively little to meet the needs of tomorrow.

Plans for the future on the part of business are reflected in the investment made by business for new plants and equipment. In 1950 this figure was 21 billion dollars; in 1960, 36 billion dollars. The total for all new construction in 1950 was 30 billion dollars; in 1960, 56 billion dollars. The total for new construction for education in 1950 was 1427 million dollars, as compared with 3384 million dollars in 1960.

In 1950 corporate profits were 23 billion dollars and in 1960 this figure was exactly the same, but the amount of corporate dividends paid grew from 9 billion dollars in 1950 to 14 billion dollars in 1960.

These figures suggest that the high school graduate of 1960 lived in an expanding economy that continually made more resources and materials available to an increasing population. The impact on the individual is suggested by the figures revealing personal and family incomes. In 1950 the average family-personal income after federal taxes was 4070 dollars; in 1960 this figure was 6160 dollars. These figures in constant dollars amount to 4903 dollars in 1950 and 5620 in 1960. The net spendable weekly earning of production workers in 1950 was $50.26 as compared with $72.57 in 1960.

The actual number of wage and salaried workers in nonagricultural employment in 1950 were 45,200,000; in 1960, 54,300,000. This increase of almost 9 million workers accompanied an increase in the number of unemployed, which grew from 3,351,000 in 1950 to 3,931,000 in 1960.

One change in the nature of the working population is suggested in the reduction in number of farm households. In 1950, 6,275,000 households were classified as farm households, as compared with 4,076,000 in 1960. Nonfarm households increased from 37,279,000 in 1950 to 48,543,000 in 1960. Two other changes indirectly influence the decisions of high school students. For scientific research in 1950 the federal

45

government spent slightly over 1 billion dollars; in 1960, over 8 billion dollars. This has influenced the attitudes of many persons toward science, and the functioning of many institutions of higher learning. More directly influencing the high school senior is the change in the cost per year of attending college. In 1950 the average student could expect to pay $1100 in a private institution and $900 in a public institution. The cost of college attendance over the ten-year period increased by almost 50 per cent.

The high school senior of 1960 lived in a world quite different from that of the student in 1950. There were more people, increasing numbers resulting in new pressures. The economy grew over the decade, but so did the demands made on the economy, and the expectations of Americans grew faster than the material resources of the country. As the nation more firmly than ever before committed itself to education, higher education came to be regarded more and more as a national asset rather than a class luxury. Scientific developments such as atomic power, military activities such as the Korean War, social changes such as racial integration and desegregation, and industrial developments such as automation — all made the world a different place and all significantly influenced students as they approached their first major decisions.

CHANGES IN STUDENTS

Students in 1960 differed from their predecessors of 1950. Careful examination of two somewhat similar students from these two eras may clarify some of the changes over the decade and suggest how these changes have influenced boys and girls.

Michael Bailey, 1950. In January of 1950 Michael Bailey was a seventeen-year-old high school senior who would reach his eighteenth birthday a few days before graduation. A strong, husky, sociable young man, his speech and behavior suggested to the interviewer that he had been a life-time reader of the *American Boy.*

Michael's father, a foreman in a manufacturing plant, had completed the eighth grade. Michael had spent but little time discussing his post-high-school plans with his father and reported that Mr. Bailey had shown little enthusiasm for college: "He doesn't think college would be much good. He doesn't understand about it and thinks it is a waste of time or something."

46

Michael's mother, a housewife, was a high school graduate. Michael reported that she knew relatively little about college and had no particular desire for Michael to attend. He told the interviewer that if he went to college he would have to pay all his own expenses. The other member of Michael's immediate family was his older married sister who had completed the eleventh grade.

Michael had been a good student in high school and his scores on college aptitude tests suggested that he had enough ability to succeed academically in most colleges. In his high school, a large metropolitan school with a good academic reputation, his grades placed him within the upper 12 per cent of his graduating class. On the American Council on Education Psychological Examination his percentile score showed that he did better than 63 per cent of the freshmen entering the state university, located in his city.

Michael's reaction to school varied. In junior high school he had wanted to leave school, considering it too monotonous, but he reported having enjoyed his high school work. He added that he really had not taken the right kind of courses in high school to prepare him for college since he had avoided most of the difficult academic subjects.

Michael had acquired no work experience other than chores around the neighborhood until his senior year when he took a part-time job in a store, and he enjoyed this work. He had considered a factory job as an alternative, but preferred the store. Several months before graduation he had already accepted a job in a hardware store, to begin immediately after graduation. He hoped eventually to become a sales clerk in the store.

He had considered attending college and majoring in political science, but finally decided this was too broad a course to be practical. The dean of men in his high school had told him that a major in political science would facilitate obtaining a government job, but Michael commented: "So long as I have the chance for a good job I thought I might as well take it. If I went to college I'd just go to get a diploma so I could get a good job. I feel that I don't need college now that I have a good job." He did tell the interviewer that he was contemplating a sales course at a vocational school that summer since his job at the hardware store would be only part-time until fall.

His high school principal and some of his teachers mildly encouraged

Michael to attend college. He had neglected to submit an application for a scholarship because he never got around to completing the required autobiography, and even when his principal offered to apply for a scholarship for him, Michael declined.

In general, he felt he could do quite well in the world by working up rather than by attending college. His academic and scholastic interests were not strong, his values tending to reflect the nonintellectual attitudes of his parents and immediate associates. He had enjoyed courses on modern problems and history in high school, but these had failed to provide any lasting stimulation. He had taken the minimum amount of mathematics and science and had received relatively little counseling early in high school regarding his academic planning.

Michael lived in a world and at a time that did not require him to consider his military responsibilities. A few weeks after his graduation the Korean War broke out and eventual military service became inevitable. Seven months later he decided to enlist in the Air Force rather than wait to be drafted. Early in 1950, however, military commitments appeared to influence the behaviors and attitudes of young men relatively little.

Most young men who graduated from high school in 1950 could obtain jobs easily; opportunities for employment were increasing faster than the rather small number of job seekers entering the labor market.

Although machines had been replacing men for decades, the threat of automation did not motivate most young persons to obtain further training. The world of 1950 as seen by those who lived in it was far from simple and certainly not free of problems. To the citizen of the world of 1960, however, the decisions made by students of the earlier decade appeared to be relatively simple and obvious.

John Shayne, 1960. In January of 1960 John Shayne was a high school senior who would graduate a few weeks before his eighteenth birthday. Athletic and handsome, John was popular with his classmates and well liked by his teachers. During his junior year he had decided to attend college but as yet had made no commitment to either a college or a curriculum. Mr. Shayne, a supervisor in a refinery, had completed the tenth grade. John's mother had graduated from high school, completed a six-month course in a business college, and a few years earlier, when John's only brother had reached the age of fourteen, had accepted a part-time office job.

Tests of general intelligence and scholastic achievement during John's sojourn in school had continuously demonstrated his superior intellectual ability and excellent background of educational information. On the Minnesota Scholastic Aptitude Test his score exceeded the scores of 69 per cent of freshmen in the arts college of his state university and his high school grades placed him within the upper 15 per cent of his class. From early years in junior high school he had opportunities to discuss with counselors his abilities and interests, and at least once a year during his time in elementary school one or both of his parents had conferences with his teachers. Twice while John was in junior high school and twice while he was in senior high school his school counselor met with John and his parents to discuss his educational and vocational plans.

Over the years both of John's parents became increasingly convinced of the desirability of John's attending college. Although they provided some encouragement and moral support, they could offer little intellectual or academic stimulation at home and they were unable to promise John substantial financial assistance. Mr. Shayne was willing to have John live at home if he attended a local college, and thus relieve him of the cost of board and room, but because of the family's limited income little cash assistance could be provided.

John had earned money while in high school caring for neighbors' lawns, caddying at a nearby golf course, and for a few weeks during the summers working as a carry-out boy in a supermarket. Several times he had looked for regular work after school or during summers, but the only jobs available were so far from his home that the cost and problems of transportation made these jobs unfeasible.

In high school John had taken three years of mathematics and one science course. He had discontinued study of a foreign language after a year's effort because of barely passing grades.

Although no persons in John's family and few in the families of his friends had attended college, most were high school graduates, and most of his friends were planning to continue their education beyond high school. The few boys John knew who had graduated from high school in previous years and decided to enter the labor market immediately

49

either had great difficulty finding employment or had been unable to find jobs that offered opportunity and that they considered interesting.

Although he had never found it compellingly interesting, John had never seriously considered leaving school. In the eleventh grade one of his teachers who taught a combined course in English and social studies had provided more intellectual stimulation than John had previously experienced, and he hoped his teachers in college would resemble Mr. Thomas.

John planned to work the summer after graduation and accumulate enough money for his tuition. Although he had no job in sight he felt sure that because of his muscular physique and the recommendations he could expect from his school that he would be able to get a laboring job, perhaps with a construction crew. His counselor had told him about financial resources available to students, particularly loan funds under the National Defense Education Act, and John and his family had accepted the idea that higher education could be financed with borrowed funds. Some of John's friends already attending college had informed him about employment opportunities for students, and the Shayne family thought that any financial obstacles could be overcome.

John and his family had discussed with the school counselor his obligation for military service and had decided that if John entered the university or another college where training for the Reserve Officer Training Corps was available John would enlist in the ROTC. All agreed that every effort should be made for John to complete his college work before entering military service.

Although undecided on a vocation, John had enjoyed his experiences in working with younger persons and was seriously considering obtaining a degree in education. His parents encouraged this choice, his father believing that teachers would always be needed and were guaranteed a fairly comfortable standard of living. From discussions with his counselor, John was aware that teachers of English and social studies tended to exceed the number of available jobs whereas teachers of mathematics and science were in great demand. In the light of his performance in mathematics he was considering this field as a possibility.

John, in 1960, was making decisions in a world where the process of change was constantly being accelerated. This country was highly industrialized and highly militarized. Unemployment rates were high among the unskilled and uneducated, but great manpower shortages existed in occupations requiring specialized education. Each year the general educational level of the community advanced, accompanied by increasing acceptance of the need for education.

John's schools had accepted the responsibility for providing careful counseling and had given John and his parents repeated opportunities for studying his potential, his needs, his opportunities, and his alternatives. The nation and the community were constantly increasing the absolute and the relative amount of money spent on education, particularly on higher education.

Not only did the conditions and influences affecting Michael and John change over the decade, but — equally important — the awareness of these influences changed. John and his parents perhaps achieved a better understanding of John's needs and of the conditions affecting his decisions than did either Michael or his parents. The two boys lived in different worlds, with different kinds of persons, and made different decisions.

FUTURE TRENDS

Many of the changes and trends beginning in the decade from 1950 to 1960 will be accelerated between 1960 and 1970. Young people born during the great postwar baby boom, successively swamping the elementary schools, the junior highs, and the high schools, began to graduate from high school in 1964. Not only will the number of young people reaching the age of eighteen greatly increase but the proportion of the age group graduating from high school will also be larger because of the attacks being made upon the school dropout problem.

As these students complete high school, many of them will be unable to find jobs. Although the nation's economy may continue to expand, it will not expand rapidly enough to prevent a serious unemployment problem among those young people. The fact that there is a high unemployment rate among the unskilled and untrained, while shortages of trained manpower exist in many specialized areas, will not be ignored by either students or parents in the mid-1960's. The demand for further training beyond high school, both collegiate and noncollegiate, will grow rapidly as the proportion of graduates directly entering the labor market continues to decrease and the proportion continuing their edu-

51

cation increases. Many types of high school student, who even in 1960 did not plan on college, will be making such plans in 1965. Meeting the needs of these increased numbers of young people seeking training will be one of the major problems confronting American college educators during the next decade.

4

Two Surveys Eleven Years Apart

ALTHOUGH the information in this report is derived primarily from the high school graduates of 1961, in some chapters these students are compared with those of more than a decade earlier. The purpose of the study is to provide a description of the current generation of high school graduates in Minnesota as well as a basis for inferences about changes over the intervening eleven years. The present chapter deals more directly with comparisons between the two generations of 1950 and 1961.

Several questions are relevant. How do the two generations differ? To what extent did the proportions of each plan group of high school seniors change over the eleven years? To what extent did changes occur in the relationship between these plans and such variables as sex, area, socioeconomic status, and ability? What are possible reasons for the changes observed, and what are the implications of these changes?

CHANGES IN PLANS

In 1950, 24,892 or approximately 95 per cent of all twelfth-grade students in Minnesota's public and private schools completed a questionnaire reporting their plans for the year following high school graduation. Similar questionnaires were completed by 44,756 (97 per cent) seniors from the graduating class of 1961. This is an 80 per cent increase in the number of seniors, consisting of both increases in numbers of persons this age and greater proportions of the age group completing high school. From 1950 through 1960 Minnesota's population increased from 2,982,483 to 3,413,864, or 14.5 per cent.

Table 4 shows the percentage of students by sex and area expressing

Table 4. Percentage Distribution of Seniors with Different Post-High-School Plans, by Sex and Area

| | Boys | | | | | | | | Girls | | | | | | | | Total | |
| | Metro. | | Non-farm | | Farm | | Total | | Metro. | | Non-farm | | Farm | | Total | | | |
	'50	'61	'50	'61	'50	'61	'50	'61	'50	'61	'50	'61	'50	'61	'50	'61	'50	'61
Get a job	30	12	32	15	28	21	30	15	41	30	38	29	46	40	41	32	36	24
Work for parents	2	1	4	2	35	15	12	5	0	0	1	0	4	1	2	0	7	3
Go to college	50	54	43	48	20	28	39	45	40	45	37	38	24	25	34	37	36	41
Go to trade school	7	8	7	8	6	9	7	8	1	3	2	5	2	5	1	4	4	6
Go to business school	2	1	3	2	2	2	2	2	6	6	8	8	8	9	8	7	5	5
Go to other school	2	1	2	1	2	1	2	1	4	3	4	5	5	5	5	4	3	3
Military service	5	17	8	20	5	20	6	18	0	1	1	1	1	1	1	1	3	9
Nursing	0	0	0	0	0	0	0	0	5	6	7	8	7	8	6	7	3	4
Other	2	6	1	4	1	5	2	5	2	6	2	6	3	6	2	6	2	6
Total	100	100	100	100	99	100	100	99	99	100	100	100	100	100	100	100	99	101

each of the several post-high-school plans. Total size of each subgroup is given in Table 5. In 1950 more than one third of Minnesota high school graduates planned to obtain jobs during the following year. Eleven years later this proportion was less than one quarter. The percentage of boys graduating from high school who planned to obtain jobs dropped from 30 to 15 per cent. Thus in spite of an almost doubling of the number of male high school graduates, the absolute number of boys planning to enter the labor market immediately after graduation was somewhat less in 1961 than in 1950. Among the girls, although the relative number planning to seek jobs dropped by more than one fifth, the absolute number of young women planning to enter the labor market actually increased by more than 1500.

Table 5. Number of Seniors with Different Plans, by Sex and Area

Area	Boys		Girls		Boys and Girls	
	1950	1961	1950	1961	1950	1961
Metropolitan	3,881	8,267	4,405	8,095	8,286	16,362
Nonfarm	4,201	7,917	4,873	8,400	9,074	16,317
Farm	3,297	6,022	4,235	6,055	7,532	12,077
Total	11,379	22,206	13,513	22,550	24,892	44,756

The percentage of students planning to work for their parents dropped markedly. Almost all of these students both in 1950 and in 1961 lived on farms and were boys. In 1950 of all boys graduated from high school and living on farms, slightly over one third planned to work for their parents. In 1961 only 15 per cent had such plans. In Minnesota opportunities on family farms either are becoming increasingly restricted or are attracting fewer and fewer farm boys. The total number of males engaged in farming in Minnesota in 1950 was 232,721, compared with 159,035 in 1960, a 32 per cent decrease.

The largest percentage increase in the number of students making plans for their post-high-school careers occurred among the boys planning to enter military service. In 1950, after World War II and before the Korean War, only 6 per cent of the boys planned to enter military service the year following high school graduation whereas the percentage in 1961 was 18. The proportion of metropolitan boys with these plans increased slightly more than threefold; the proportion of nonfarm boys increased less than threefold; and the proportion of farm boys increased fourfold.

Changes in the proportions of graduates planning post-high-school education, though large and significant, were not as large as the changes in the proportions planning to enter military service or to obtain jobs. The proportion planning to attend college over the eleven-year period increased on the average by half a percentage point per year; 36 per cent in 1950 planned to attend college, 41 per cent in 1961. Rate of increase here was slightly greater among the boys than among the girls, and for boys the rate of increase was slightly greater among those from farms than among those from other areas. Since the percentage of farm boys planning to attend college in 1950 was much lower than the percentage among boys from other areas, the meaning of this comparison is ambiguous.

Differences found in 1950 among the three groups of male students persisted in 1961. Proportionately more metropolitan boys planned to attend college than did nonfarm boys and in turn many more nonfarm boys planned to attend college than did farm boys. The same area differences were found among the girls. In 1950 among the farm students more girls than boys planned to attend college, 20 per cent of the boys and 24 per cent of the girls. In 1961, however, the sex difference was reversed and more boys than girls planned to attend college, 28 per cent as compared with 25 per cent.

Both in 1950 and in 1961, where a student lived and the sex of the student were related to his plan for higher education.

Significant increases occurred in the proportions of boys and girls planning to attend trade school. Increases were relatively small for the metropolitan and nonfarm boys but larger for the farm boys. For the girls, increases were considerably larger, although only 4 per cent were planning on trade school.

The proportions planning to attend business school remained relatively constant for both sexes. In 1950, 5 per cent of the students were planning on business training; the percentage in 1961 was exactly the same.

The proportion of girls planning to enter nurses' training increased slightly from 1950 to 1961. In the earlier year 6 per cent had such plans, compared with 7 per cent eleven years later. Again it must be remarked

56

that although the percentage increase was small, these girls increased in number from approximately 800 to approximately 1600. With an increase of one percentage point in the proportion of girls planning to enter nursing, the actual number with such plans about doubled.

In summary, the eleven-year period was marked by significant changes in the plans of high school graduates. Far fewer students in 1961 planned to obtain jobs; far fewer farm boys planned to work for their parents; many more boys planned to enter military service; the proportion of students planning to enter college increased considerably, as did the proportion planning on other training programs. Sex and area differences observed in 1950 persisted in 1961 with a notable shift occurring among farm boys and girls planning to attend college: college was a more popular plan among farm girls in 1950, and in 1961 more popular among farm boys.

CHARACTERISTICS OF SENIORS

In considering the post-high-school plans of Minnesota seniors and the changes in conditions related to these plans, it is useful to examine the entire population of high school seniors and note the changes which occurred between the classes over the eleven years.

Age. The 1961 high school graduates were more homogeneous in age than their predecessors in 1950. Only 2 per cent of the 1961 students were sixteen years of age, compared with 7 per cent of the 1950 seniors. One per cent were nineteen or older, compared with 2.5 per cent in 1950. Most students — 82 per cent — were seventeen, 14 per cent were eighteen years of age. Significantly fewer students, it appears, were either accelerated or held back during their school careers in the 1961 group as compared with the students of 1950.

Father's Occupation. Type of occupation in which their fathers were engaged was reported by Minnesota's high school seniors of 1961 as shown in the accompanying tabulation. In 1950 only 16 per cent were

Type of Occupation	%	Type of Occupation	%
Professions	6	Factory worker	15
Owns or manages business	13	Other	9
Office work	4	Deceased or disabled	3
Sales	5	Retired or pensioned	1
Owns or manages farm	20	Unemployed	0.4
Skilled trade	19	No answer	3

57

in skilled trades and 27 per cent were farmers. Otherwise there were no changes.

Family Income. Social changes are also reflected in the descriptions of how the family obtains its income. Professional fees or business profits (including profits from farms) were cited by 32 per cent of the 1961 seniors; fixed salary by 23 per cent; wages by 36 per cent; investments by 1 per cent; and pensions by 3 per cent.

The proportion checking "fees or business profits" showed a decrease of 8 per cent from 1950, while the percentage reporting wages increased by 5 percentage points. Inclusion of profits from farms in the "fees or business profits" category may be the reason why this proportion has diminished, and movement to towns and cities has increased the proportion obtaining income from hourly or daily wages.

Education of Parents. Parents of the 1961 seniors were significantly better educated than those of the 1950 seniors. Large differences occurred in the educational levels of both parents among families living in different residence areas. Changes related to fathers' education are shown in Table 6. The changes which occurred in the metropolitan area consisted

Table 6. Percentage Distribution of Boys on the Basis of
Father's Education, for 1950 and 1961

Amount of Education	Area					
	Metropolitan		Nonfarm		Farm	
	1950	1961	1950	1961	1950	1961
Did not attend school	0	0	0	0	0	0
Some grade school	9	3	12	6	21	11
Completed eighth grade	24	16	33	31	50	55
Some high school	15	15	14	13	11	11
Graduated from high school	16	26	12	23	6	14
Business or trade school	11	10	10	7	6	4
Some college work (including						
teacher training)	6	9	4	6	2	2
College graduate	10	12	8	8	2	1
Holds more than one college degree ..	4	5	3	3	0	0
No answer	3	3	3	2	2	1

of considerably more fathers having graduated from high school or having some high school training. The same trend was recorded for the nonfarm area, but the changes were smaller, while for the farm area the shifts were from less than an eighth-grade education to completion of the eighth grade, and from less than a high school education to high school graduation. For the 1961 groups, one fifth from the metropolitan area, slightly over a third from the nonfarm area, and approximately two thirds from the farm area had fathers who had completed no more than an eighth-grade education.

Similar changes were found for the educational level of the mothers, although there were considerable differences between fathers and mothers in actual levels achieved. The percentages of mothers who had some college education were similar to those reported for fathers. The mothers, however, were more likely than fathers to have continued their education only to the point of high school graduation. For example, 34 per cent of the 1961 seniors reported that the highest level of education achieved by their mothers was getting a high school diploma, as compared with 21 per cent for fathers. Thirty-nine per cent of the students reported their fathers had an eighth-grade education or less, as compared with 26 per cent of their mothers.

The proportions of boys and girls graduating from high school are now equal, while the proportion of boys obtaining some college education is higher than that for girls. A study of Minnesota high school seniors undertaken twenty to twenty-five years from now should show equal proportions of mothers and fathers graduating from high school, and a higher proportion of fathers with some college education.

Family Income. No differences in adequacy of family income were reported by the students over the eleven-year period. For both 1950 and 1961 seniors, the data are reported in Table 7. The two groups differed in the percentages of students not going to college who said they would change their plans and attend if they had more money. In 1950, 28 per

Table 7. Family Income as Described by Percentages of Total Group

Category	1950 (N = 25,040)	1961 (N = 44,754)
Frequently have difficulty making ends meet	4	5
Sometimes have difficulty in getting the necessities	4	6
Have all the necessities but not many luxuries	24	24
Comfortable but not well-to-do	59	57
Well-to-do	7	7
Wealthy	0.25	0.20
No response	3	1

59

cent said they would change their plans, as compared with 24 per cent in 1961. Reported lack of finances, then, appeared to be slightly less of a barrier to college attendance than previously. Of those who said they would attend college if they had more money, the amount reported as needed remained the same as compared with 1950. Twelve per cent said they would need enough for all of their college expenses; 13 per cent, enough for half; and 2 per cent, enough for less than half.

Description of Home. The seniors of both years were asked about the presence of various appliances and conveniences in their homes. In 1950 these items significantly differentiated between students who were and students who were not planning to go to college. By 1961 the same appliances and conveniences were found in most homes and were not related to college plans.

The same proportion, 80 per cent, reported family ownership of their homes in 1950 as in 1961. In 1950, 79 per cent reported that their homes had central heating, and this proportion increased to 90 per cent in 1961. The largest increase was found among the farm students, where the percentage reporting central heating increased from 62 to 78 per cent. Ninety-four per cent of the seniors reported running water, as compared with 81 per cent in 1950. Again the largest increase occurred among students from the farm, where the increase was from 50 to 83 per cent. In 1950, 40 per cent of the farm students reported both hot and cold running water, and this percentage increased to 77 per cent in 1961. In 1950, 84 per cent of the seniors said that their homes had electric and gas refrigerators, but this appliance was found in only 74 per cent of the farm homes. In 1961 an electric or gas refrigerator was found in the homes of more than 99 per cent of the students from all residence areas.

Ninety-three per cent of the students reported a telephone in the home in 1961, as compared with 85 per cent in 1950. Again the largest increase occurred in the farm homes, from 70 to 85 per cent. In 1950, 45 per cent of the students reported that their family owned or rented a deep freeze unit or locker. In 1961 this proportion had risen to 66 per cent. The largest increase occurred in the metropolitan group, where the proportion rose from about a quarter of the homes in 1950 to about half in 1961. A deep freeze was available to 91 per cent of the families from farms. In 1950, 10 per cent of the farm homes were without electric lights, and this percentage decreased to less than 1 per cent in 1961.

In 1950 television was found in only 6 per cent of the homes of the graduating seniors. By 1961 only 6 per cent were *without* television sets. Television sets are now found in 99 per cent of the metropolitan, 95 per cent of the nonfarm, and 89 per cent of the farm homes of students. Some families in metropolitan areas do not have television, but only rarely are they families with teenagers.

Size of Home. In reporting the number of persons living in their homes, the 1950 and 1961 graduating seniors were similar. In 1961, 2 per cent of the seniors reported two people living in the home; 17 per cent reported three; 25 per cent reported four; 21 per cent reported five; 14 per cent reported six; 8 per cent reported seven; 5 per cent reported eight; 3 per cent reported nine; 2 per cent reported ten; and 2 per cent reported eleven or more.

In 1961 the percentages coming from homes of nine, ten, and eleven or more rooms were slightly larger, and the percentages reporting homes with fewer than five rooms were slightly smaller. Of the 1961 seniors 53 per cent had a bedroom to themselves, as compared with 49 per cent in 1950.

Books and Magazines in the Home. Although the number of appliances and television sets in the homes of the seniors increased dramatically over the decade, the number of books and magazines reported remained substantially the same. The number of books increased slightly, with only about a fifth of the seniors reporting fewer than twenty-five books in the home as compared with 28 per cent in 1950, while the proportion reporting more than one hundred books increased from 23 to 27 per cent. The proportion reporting the *Reader's Digest* in their homes remained the same, 53 per cent. *Life* decreased from 32 to 29 per cent, while the *Saturday Evening Post* and *Look* both increased from 22 to 28 per cent. *Time* remained the same at 15 per cent, while *Newsweek* increased from 9 to 13 per cent. The proportion reporting the *Atlantic Monthly* decreased from 4 to 2 per cent, while the figure for *Harper's* remained the same, 2 per cent. These figures imply that the reading habits of the families of high school seniors did not change much between 1950 and 1961.

Parents' Organizations. The percentages of students reporting their parents belonged to various organizations remained similar over the eleven-year period with a few impressive exceptions. Those reporting their parents belonged to the PTA increased from 39 to 49 per cent. Those reporting their parents belonged to a labor union increased from 17 to 22 per cent, while those whose mothers belonged to the Ladies' Aid decreased from 36 to 27 per cent. Organizations for which percentages remained substantially the same included the American Legion and VFW, 12 per cent; Knights of Columbus, 8 per cent; Masons, 7 per cent; Eastern Star, 4 per cent; Chamber of Commerce, 6 per cent; and sportsmen's clubs, 9 per cent.

High School Background. In 1961, 39 per cent of the graduates said they took a college preparatory course in high school, an increase of 8 percentage points over the 31 per cent reporting this curriculum in 1950. This difference matched the 8 per cent fewer students who reported they took a general course in high school; 30 per cent reported this curriculum in 1961 as compared with 38 per cent in 1950. Other types of courses remained the same over the eleven-year period: 7 per cent in a technical curriculum, 18 per cent in a commercial curriculum, and 3 per cent in an agricultural curriculum.

The students were asked to check the reasons for taking the high school curriculum they were completing, and examination of these reasons explains some of the changes which have occurred. More students went to college in 1961 than in 1950 — 41 per cent as compared with 36 per cent. More variety of curriculums was offered in the high schools in 1961. In 1950, 9 per cent of the graduates checked the reason, "it was the only one offered," while in 1961 this proportion dropped to 4 per cent. In 1961, 14 per cent of the graduates checked "advice of counselor" as an important reason why they took the curriculum they did, as compared with only 6 per cent in 1950. Fifty-one per cent of the 1961 graduates checked that the course fitted their vocational plans the best, as compared with 44 per cent in 1950, and 21 per cent checked "parent's advice" as an important reason, a significant increase over the 14 per cent checking this reason in 1950. Other percentages which showed no change over the last decade included: teacher's advice, 6 per cent; required by school, 8 per cent; seemed easiest, 4 per cent; was best in this type of course, 17 per cent; found it the most interesting, 33 per cent.

Seventeen per cent of students not planning to attend college the year following graduation said they were planning to attend at a later date. Seven per cent planned to attend after one year, 4 per cent after two years, 3 per cent after three years, and 3 per cent after four or more years. It is difficult to estimate just what proportion of these students will actually carry out these plans, but if only half of them do, the total proportion of the graduating seniors who attend college will fall somewhere between 45 and 50 per cent.

Marriage and Plans. The 1961 graduates were asked if marriage or the early prospect of marriage influenced their plans for the coming year. Only 11 per cent of them — 6 per cent of the boys and 17 per cent of the girls — answered in the affirmative. They were also asked if they had any idea when they planned to get married. One third of 1 per cent of each of the sexes reported they were already married, and 4 per cent of the girls and .5 per cent of the boys indicated plans for marriage shortly after graduation. Another 5 per cent of the girls and 1 per cent of the boys stated they planned to be married the second year after graduation from high school. Ninety per cent of the girls and 98 per cent of the boys either had no plans at all for marriage or else were not planning to be married for at least several years. Marriage, then, is not an important determinant of post-high-school plans for the vast majority of Minnesota's high school graduates. These results are consistent with several other data which have shown that the trend toward early marriage in the United States has not been felt in Minnesota to the extent that it has in other areas.

5

A Follow-Up One Year after Graduation

IN 1951 a follow-up survey of a sample of the 1950 graduates was conducted to determine to what extent the plans made by these students in the middle of their senior year were actually fulfilled during the following year. Although many students changed their plans, the over-all proportions of students actually pursuing the various plans were close to the proportions of those who had chosen these plans the year before. Conditions in 1961 differed considerably from those of a decade earlier, and although it was expected that the over-all "realizability" of plans would be essentially the same as for 1950, a similar follow-up survey was conducted in the late spring of 1962.

When compared with the total sample in regard to sex and plans, the respondents were found to be representative of the entire group, although a slightly larger proportion had planned originally on college. This difference was not statistically significant, however. The respondents had higher MSAT scores than did the total sample; the mean MSAT score of the nonrespondents was approximately one half a standard deviation below that of the respondents. The somewhat larger proportion of respondents who had originally planned on college was in part accounted for by the larger proportion of college-going metropolitan students responding to the follow-up questionnaire. Unlocatable students proved to be somewhat atypical in their plans, but their numbers were not large enough to bias the returns significantly. The original plans and the activities actually undertaken by these respondents of the follow-up inquiry are shown in Table 8.

64

Table 8. Percentage Distribution of Original Plans and Activities Actually Undertaken by 1683 Follow-Up Respondents

	Boys								Girls								Total	
	Metro.		Nonfarm		Farm		Total		Metro.		Nonfarm		Farm		Total			
Alternatives	Plan	Act.	Plan	Act.	Plan	Act.	Plan	Act.	Plan	Act.	Plan	Act.	Plan	Act.	Plan	Act.	Plan	Act.
Get a job	11	21	12	16	25	27	14	21	27	39	29	36	38	49	30	40	22	30
Work for parents	0	0	2	1	13	17	3	4	0	0	0	0	0	2	0	1	2	2
College	60	56	54	53	27	28	51	50	50	45	43	37	29	26	44	39	48	44
Trade school	7	4	8	6	10	7	8	5	4	3	4	4	4	4	4	3	6	4
Business school	1	2	0	2	2	0	1	1	5	3	5	5	12	5	6	4	4	3
Other school	0	0	1	0	1	0	1	0	3	1	3	1	4	2	3	1	2	1
Marriage									2	4	1	6	2	8	2	5	1	2
Nursing									4	3	13	8	8	2	7	4	4	2
Military	12	15	18	22	18	19	15	18									8	9
Other	8	2	5	1	3	2	6	2	5	3	1	2	4	1	4	2	5	2

FOLLOW-UP RESULTS

Comparisons of original plans and actual activities show that in 1961, as in 1950, the proportions of students with various high school plans are rough indicators of the actual proportions of students who will be entering the activities related to these plans. A smaller proportion of girls actually attended college than had originally planned to, and a larger proportion of students had jobs than had planned to seek employment. On the follow-up questionnaire the students were asked to check their "major activity" during the past year. Some students apparently attended short business or vocational courses before getting jobs and therefore reported that their major activity was "working." This could help account for the slightly lower proportion reporting trade and business schools in the follow-up study and also for the higher proportion working. A few of the working students were undoubtedly a part of the group which enters college each fall but drops out during the first few months. As a whole, the differences in proportion between students actually entering the various activities and students who had planned to enter them were similar to those found in 1950.

Furthermore, the over-all "realizability" of the plans of the 1961 seniors did not differ greatly from the corresponding figure in 1950 — 67 per cent in 1961 versus 64 per cent in 1950. The over-all extent to which both sexes fulfilled their plans was not significantly different for these 1961 seniors. Significantly fewer of the farm students, however, 59 per cent, fulfilled their plans than did students from the metropolitan area, 68 per cent, and the nonfarm area, 71 per cent. The extent to which the different groups fulfilled their plans of the previous year is shown in Table 9.

Although a third of the respondents did not fulfill the plans they had made midway in their senior year, as mentioned above, the proportions who finally ended up in the various activities corresponded quite closely to the proportions originally making such plans.

The extent to which different plans were realized varied. While 84 per cent of the students who said they were planning on college actually entered college, only 20 per cent who planned to attend business school actually did so. A few more percentage points probably should be added to this figure to account for the students who took only short courses in business school. While 84 per cent of the students planning on college

Table 9. Percentage of Students Who Followed Original Plans

Original Plan	Boys				Girls				Total
	Metro.	Non-farm	Farm	Total	Metro.	Non-farm	Farm	Total	
Get a job	58	62	55	58	85	77	74	80	73
Work for parents ..	0	25	57	52	0	0	0	0	48
College	87	89	77	86	83	80	83	82	84
Trade school	26	53	44	38	47	44	67	50	42
Business school ...	17	0	0	9	14	42	21	23	20
Other school	0	50	0	20	0	12	14	8	10
Military service ...	51	74	47	57					57
Nursing					26	52	31	39	39
Marriage					71	100	100	85	85
Other	0	0	0	0	0	0	14	3	1
N	312	157	97	566	301	158	102	561	1,127

actually entered college, 91 per cent of those who actually entered had originally planned to do so. Marriage was the plan most frequently fulfilled for the girls, since 11 of the 13 girls who had originally so planned did get married. On the other hand, of the 42 girls who reported they were married and not engaged in any other major activity at the time of the follow-up study, only 11 of them, or 26 per cent, had expressed any intention of marriage on their original questionnaire. The percentage of students following their original plan to enter the military service was also lower than might be expected. There appeared to be considerable interchange between the plans and actual activities of those students planning on either jobs or military service. Twenty-three per cent of those who had planned on entering the service obtained jobs instead, and 20 per cent of those planning on jobs went into the military service. These figures of 23 and 20 per cent represent about a half of the students who in each case did not carry out their original intentions.

This investigation of what happened to those who did not fulfill their original plans revealed some interesting findings. For the most part, the activities they entered generally tended to be either logical substitutes or possible steppingstones to the fulfillment of their original intentions. Among the girls, most who planned to but did not get a job got married, and the majority of those who planned on business school actually got jobs. Among the boys, in addition to the changes regarding jobs and military service, about 5 per cent of those who intended to enter college instead found jobs. On the other hand, 7 per cent of those planning on a job found themselves in college.

Particular attention was paid to the 125 students in the follow-up group who did not act on their plans to enter college. Of these students not attending college the year after graduation, 37, or 30 per cent, stated on the follow-up questionnaire that they intended to go to college the following year. Since almost all of these students were working, it is reasonable to assume that many of them found it necessary to accumulate some savings before they were able to continue their education. The remaining 88 persons in this group apparently either had given up their college aspirations altogether, or at least did not anticipate entering college for some time.

The 125 students who did not follow their college plans were compared with the 677 persons who did on a number of the original questionnaire variables: education of mother and father, MSAT scores, description of family's economic status, influence of marriage on plans, reasons for making original plans, family's attitude toward college attendance, and number of books in the home. Fulfillment of college plans was found to be significantly related to parental education for the metropolitan students. Twenty-five per cent of the fathers of students following their college plans had one or more college degrees, compared with only 7 per cent of the fathers of the noncollege-going group. The corresponding figures for the mothers' education were 16 and 3 per cent, respectively. Among the nonmetropolitan groups differences were in the same direction but were statistically significant only in the case of the mothers' education.

Description of family economic status was not related to whether or not these students carried out their college plans, nor were the reasons given for making these plans. Those who did not get to college, however, reported significantly more often on their original questionnaires that marriage or the early prospect of marriage had influenced their planning.

How their families felt about their college plans also differentiated significantly between the two groups, and as would be expected, those who did not fulfill their plans reported more often that their families were indifferent or did not want them to go, and less often that their families wanted or insisted that they go.

Among the nonmetropolitan students of both sexes, the number of books in the home was reported to be significantly higher for students fulfilling their plans than for those not doing so. Among the metropolitan students differences on this variable approached but did not meet the .05 per cent level of statistical significance.

The college aptitude of the two groups, as measured by the Minnesota Scholastic Aptitude Test, differed considerably. The mean MSAT score of those following their plans was 40.9, nearly a full standard deviation above the 32.6 mean score achieved by the college-bound students not following their plans. Only 31 per cent of the noncollege-attending group exceeded the median score of entering freshmen at the University of Minnesota, whereas 57 per cent of the college planners who attended did so. The difference between means was not only highly statistically significant ($t = 7.11$), but was also large enough to be of considerable practical significance.

SUMMARY

The "realizability" of the plans made by graduating high school students midway in their senior year has not changed a great deal since 1950, in spite of substantial changes in prevailing conditions. Even though only 67 per cent of the students actually followed the plans they made as seniors, the actual proportions of students entering various activities corresponded closely with the proportions making these plans.

Certain types of plans tended to be fulfilled to a far greater extent than other types. More students who were planning on college fulfilled their intentions than did those who made other plans. Most of the students planning on college whose abilities and home environments appeared conducive to college attendance went to college. Those with college plans who were similar in background to most college students went to college, in contrast to students with college plans who in background and other characteristics tended to resemble students who got jobs. Many high school seniors who did not follow their plans immediately still intended to do so, but not until after a year or more following graduation.

6

Ability and College Attendance

THE previous chapter reported that the numbers as well as the proportion of high school graduates entering college have increased significantly over the past decade. Many persons interested in higher education have become alarmed about these large increases, fearful that more students of lower ability must be included now that "everybody" is attending college. This, they assert, naturally results in a watered-down, less vigorous, and less intellectual experience for the more talented students who formerly had the campuses to themselves.

If from the study of the achievement and aptitude records of high school seniors we find that lower ability students have shown a greater proportionate increase in college attendance than higher ability students, then these worries could have some validity. If, on the other hand, proportions at all levels of ability have increased equally, or if, conversely, proportions of high ability students show a greater increase than those with less ability, then these fears, at least in reference to the past decade, would be groundless.

Information about the ability and high school achievement of seniors was available from the State-Wide Testing Program sponsored by the Association of Minnesota Colleges and administered by the Student Counseling Bureau of the University of Minnesota. As a part of this program all juniors in all public and private high schools in the state take a scholastic aptitude test in January of their junior year. In the past, the test administered was the American Council on Education Psychological Examination (ACE); since 1958 the Minnesota Scholastic Aptitude Test (MSAT), a condensed version of the Ohio Psychological Test, has been used. Each high school in the state also reports to the

Student Counseling Bureau the rank in class of each of the juniors in that high school as of the end of the junior year. The Student Counseling Bureau then computes the percentile rank in high school class and the percentile score for the MSAT and reports these data for each student to the high school and to all colleges in the association. Of the 44,756 students who completed the questionnaire in this study, information regarding scholastic aptitude and high school achievement was available for 42,078. Those for whom information was not available were students who had moved at some time during the end of their junior or first half of their senior year, or who, for one reason or another, missed the junior year testing.

MINNESOTA SCHOLASTIC APTITUDE TEST SCORES

The means and standard deviations of MSAT scores obtained by the students in the study are shown in Table 10. The mean for metropolitan students is higher than that for nonfarm students and this mean is higher than that for the farm students. In each case women obtained higher means than men. Each of these differences is statistically significant at or beyond the .001 probability level, although with the exception of lower mean scores among farm groups, the differences are not large enough to have practical significance.

The range of MSAT scores was divided into deciles for students in this study and those within each of these deciles were compared according to post-high-school plan. The results are shown in Table 11 for the boys and in Table 12 for the girls. In examining the results in these tables the information regarding differences in ability among the various residence areas as shown in Table 10 should be kept in mind. For example, an MSAT raw score equal to a percentile score of 90 among the farm boys would be equal to a percentile score of 80 for the nonfarm and of 75 for the metropolitan boys.

Table 10. Mean MSAT Scores by Sex and Residence Areas

Area	Boys			Girls		
	Mean	Standard Deviation	N	Mean	Standard Deviation	N
Metropolitan	32.86	14.67	7,681	33.73	14.37	7,604
Nonfarm	30.73	13.53	7,519	32.56	13.96	7,961
Farm	26.62	14.17	5,656	29.16	12.40	5,721

Table 11. Percentage Distribution of Boys According to Area, Plan, and MSAT Decile*

MSAT Decile (approximate)	Metropolitan (Total N = 7,681)						Nonfarm (Total N = 7,519)						Farm (Total N = 5,721)					
	Job	Col.	Trd.	Bus.	Mil.	N	Job	Col.	Trd.	Bus.	Mil.	N	Job	Col.	Trd.	Bus.	Mil.	N
91–100	1	94	0	0	2	761	3	89	1	0	4	752	7	75	2	1	7	579
81–90	5	84	2	0	7	802	5	79	2	1	10	809	12	53	6	2	13	640
71–80	6	77	2	1	9	700	8	69	4	1	13	809	18	37	3	2	18	538
61–70	7	69	4	1	12	824	10	56	8	0	17	719	18	30	10	2	19	621
51–60	10	62	8	1	13	684	15	48	9	3	20	796	22	23	11	1	22	544
41–50	11	51	9	2	18	829	17	42	10	3	21	681	22	17	11	4	25	701
31–40	15	40	11	2	22	692	16	35	8	2	25	754	23	12	10	4	25	499
21–30	19	35	10	2	22	665	25	26	10	3	26	725	27	10	9	1	23	471
11–20	21	26	14	2	28	868	28	18	12	4	29	716	30	7	10	1	21	621
1–10	22	18	17	2	28	856	27	11	15	2	32	758	31	5	11	1	25	442

*Percentages within each decile do not add up to 100 because several plan groups, such as "work for parents" and "other," are not included in this table.

Table 12. Percentage Distribution of Girls According to Area, Plan, and MSAT Decile*

MSAT Decile (approximate)	Metropolitan (Total N = 7,604)						Nonfarm (Total N = 7,961)						Farm (Total N = 5,721)					
	Job	Col.	Trd.	Bus.	Nur.	N	Job	Col.	Trd.	Bus.	Nur.	N	Job	Col.	Trd.	Bus.	Nur.	N
91-100	5	80	0	1	2	732	8	79	0	3	6	835	17	60	1	5	10	625
81-90	12	74	0	2	6	791	14	66	1	4	10	786	24	47	3	7	11	599
71-80	18	65	2	4	5	749	20	53	3	6	10	803	32	34	3	9	12	552
61-70	22	59	2	4	8	783	23	45	3	8	11	879	38	25	4	10	13	542
51-60	27	48	4	5	6	758	28	38	5	8	9	846	40	21	7	12	6	544
41-50	36	38	3	6	6	752	31	29	7	9	10	891	43	20	6	13	6	598
31-40	38	31	4	8	6	858	37	24	6	10	8	707	48	14	6	12	6	617
21-30	39	28	5	9	5	642	42	16	9	11	7	745	47	11	9	9	7	433
11-20	46	19	6	10	4	824	45	13	9	9	7	828	56	8	5	8	4	619
1-10	49	12	6	10	4	715	47	8	8	10	5	641	56	4	8	9	5	592

*Percentages within each decile do not add up to 100 because several plan groups, such as "work for parents" and "other," are not included in this table.

The tables show post-high-school plans are closely related to college aptitude test scores. Eighty per cent of the students in the top decile planned to attend college as compared with 10 per cent in the bottom decile. Only 7 per cent in the top decile planned to seek jobs immediately as compared with 38 per cent in the bottom decile.

Between sexes and among geographic areas many interesting differences occur in this relationship between aptitude and plan. Among the boys in the top decile, about 90 per cent from metropolitan and nonfarm areas planned on college as compared with only 75 per cent from the farm. Among the girls this difference is 80 per cent as compared with 60 per cent of the farm girls. These same differences appear throughout the range of aptitude so that even in the lowest decile 18 per cent of the metropolitan boys are planning on college as compared with 5 per cent of the farm boys. In each decile the percentage of boys attending college is higher than that for girls, with a slight exception occurring in the lower deciles of the farm groups. For all students, the proportion in each decile planning to seek employment increases as aptitude test scores decrease. Among the boys planning to enter the military service a similar relationship to test scores is found.

A slightly smaller proportion of girls in the top decile planned to enter nursing as compared with the next two or three deciles. Below the middle decile the number entering nursing tends to decrease as scores decrease. Among girls from the farm and nonfarm areas, considerably higher proportions entering nursing were in the upper deciles as compared with the metropolitan group.

The trend among girls entering business school differs between metropolitan and nonmetropolitan groups. In the nonmetropolitan groups proportionately more business-school plans are found in the middle deciles than in the upper and lower deciles. In the metropolitan group, however, the frequency of those entering business school increases as the aptitude scores decrease.

For the considerably fewer boys entering business school, the trend among those from the metropolitan and nonfarm areas is similar to that of metropolitan girls — increasing numbers as the deciles fall. The highest frequencies of farm boys entering business school are found in the middle deciles.

Male students planning on trade school increase in numbers as scholastic aptitude scores decrease. A higher proportion of farm boys in the upper deciles enter trade school as compared with the other two male groups. A larger proportion of higher ability boys from the farm also enter the military service, as compared with the other two groups.

HIGH SCHOOL PERCENTILE RANK

The mean high school percentile ranks are shown for each of the groups in Table 13. The mean achievement ranks of the girls are considerably above those of the boys. This difference is consistent with most other studies of school achievement. The mean for the total group slightly exceeds 50 because of the method used to compute the percentile

Table 13. Mean High School Percentile Ranks by Sex and Residence Area

	Boys			Girls		
Area	Mean Per- centile Rank	Standard Devia- tion (approxi- mate)	N	Mean Per- centile Rank	Standard Devia- tion (approxi- mate)	N
Metropolitan	47.67	28.8	7,839	57.38	27.6	7,649
Nonfarm	44.69	28.8	7,557	58.27	27.6	7,851
Farm	42.30	28.8	5,707	57.39	27.5	5,745

ranks and perhaps because of selective attrition which may take place after the end of the junior year. The large differences found among the residence areas for the boys are not present for the girls. The differences between sexes in high school percentile ranks are greatest for the farm students and smallest for the metropolitan students.

Post-high-school plans by decile of high school rank are shown in Tables 14 and 15. When the figures in these tables are compared with those of the preceding ones dealing with aptitude test scores, the relationships between these two variables and post-high-school plans are found to be similar.

Approximately 90 per cent of the top decile males from all areas attend college. The lower percentage going to college in the top decile of the farm group on MSAT scores does not appear for high school rank. Farm boys are less likely than those in other areas to make the top decile of their class. If they do, however, they go to college in almost as large

Table 14. Percentage Distribution of Boys According to Area, Plan, and High School Percentile Rank*

High School Percentile Rank	Metropolitan (Total N = 7,839)						Nonfarm (Total N = 7,557)						Farm (Total N = 5,707)					
	Job	Col.	Trd.	Bus.	Mil.	N	Job	Col.	Trd.	Bus.	Mil.	N	Job	Col.	Trd.	Bus.	Mil.	N
91–100	1	95	1	0	2	657	1	93	0	0	3	548	5	88	1	1	2	259
81–90	4	85	2	0	5	663	3	87	1	0	4	539	9	69	2	2	7	373
71–80	5	80	4	0	6	703	6	78	4	0	8	618	10	54	4	1	12	429
61–70	10	69	5	1	10	705	8	72	5	1	9	642	11	45	6	2	15	522
51–60	10	60	6	1	15	808	11	57	7	3	15	726	14	35	10	3	20	561
41–50	11	55	9	2	15	802	16	46	10	2	20	811	20	24	10	2	20	639
31–40	10	44	12	2	22	878	20	38	10	3	21	854	24	17	12	3	20	669
21–30	17	38	12	2	23	954	20	27	12	4	29	897	27	12	11	2	26	743
11–20	21	26	13	2	26	890	25	18	12	2	32	961	27	7	11	1	27	758
1–10	24	19	12	3	31	779	28	11	12	2	35	961	33	3	10	1	25	754

*Percentages within each decile do not add up to 100 because several plan groups, such as "work for parents" and "other," are not included in this table.

Table 15. Percentage Distribution of Girls According to Area, Plan, and High School Percentile Rank*

High School Percentile Rank	Metropolitan (Total N = 7,649)						Nonfarm (Total N = 7,851)						Farm (Total N = 5,745)					
	Job	Col.	Trd.	Bus.	Nur.	N	Job	Col.	Trd.	Bus.	Nur.	N	Job	Col.	Trd.	Bus.	Nur.	N
91–100	10	79	1	2	5	975	10	75	0	4	7	1,054	16	59	1	8	11	693
81–90	19	67	1	3	5	968	20	57	2	5	10	1,066	27	39	3	9	12	792
71–80	24	57	1	5	5	952	20	50	4	8	10	1,014	33	36	3	7	9	677
61–70	30	47	2	7	7	899	27	38	5	10	9	888	42	22	6	8	10	705
51–60	35	40	3	6	6	850	31	31	7	9	9	818	42	19	5	13	7	624
41–50	33	38	4	6	6	731	37	25	6	10	8	776	46	13	6	12	6	560
31–40	38	26	5	9	6	693	37	21	9	9	8	664	54	7	8	10	5	497
21–30	40	22	6	8	6	643	41	13	9	8	7	618	54	7	7	9	5	447
11–20	42	20	7	8	6	523	44	10	9	10	7	523	57	4	10	6	5	425
1–10	48	15	8	9	3	415	53	3	10	7	4	430	59	4	6	6	2	325

* Percentages within each decile do not add up to 100 because several plan groups, such as "work for parents" and "other," are not included in this table.

proportions as their counterparts from the towns and cities. About 75 per cent of the girls in this top group go to college except those from the farm where the proportion drops to 60 per cent.

In the decile next to the top, the proportion going to college remains at about 85 per cent for the metropolitan and nonfarm boys but drops substantially in other groups, ranging from 69 per cent of the farm boys down to 39 per cent of the farm girls. These figures indicate that with the exception of the farm girls, most of the students whose high school achievement places them in the upper decile of their graduating class are attending college.

If it is assumed that most of the students in the decile next to the top also have the ability to profit from further education, then it becomes apparent that at this level we are losing many able students — among girls in all areas and among boys from the farm.

The proportion of students seeking jobs increases as the high school rank descends, and this trend is similar to that found for aptitude scores. The proportion of farm boys planning to work for their parents increases rapidly as we go down the top deciles but stays fairly constant in the lower half of the distribution.

The relationship of high school rank to plans for attending trade school is also similar to that found with aptitude test scores. The proportion increases as the high school rank lowers among the metropolitan and nonfarm groups but among farm boys the largest proportion is in the middle deciles with the percentages dropping off below that level.

High school ranks of girls entering nursing show an interesting trend. Among the farm girls the largest proportion entering nursing is found in the top decile. Among nonfarm girls the proportions are highest in the next-to-the-top deciles and highest among the metropolitan group in the middle deciles. The MSAT scores also showed a somewhat similar trend.

Achievement records of girls planning to attend business school also show a trend similar to that found for aptitude test scores. Higher proportions of these girls are found in the middle deciles for the farm and nonfarm groups while higher proportions are found in the lower deciles for the metropolitan group. Here again business school seems to attract brighter girls from the farm and out-state areas than from the urban and suburban areas. Among the few girls planning on marriage immediately upon graduation there is a stronger negative relationship with high school rank than was found for MSAT scores.

HIGH-ABILITY STUDENTS

The figures given in Tables 11 and 12 show clearly that the plans of high-ability students vary greatly from the remainder of the graduating class. The 1950 study gave considerable attention to such a group of able students. The ACE (1947 form) was the college aptitude test used at that time, and all students obtaining scores exceeding 120 were included in that high-ability group. A raw score of 120 on that test placed the student in approximately the upper 15 to 20 per cent of his high school class, and in the upper 25 per cent of Minnesota college freshmen as far as college aptitude is concerned. In the 1950 study, 18 per cent of the students on whom scores were available had scores of 120 or higher. A comparable group was obtained for the 1961 class by use of the MSAT raw score of 45. Seventeen per cent of the students on whom scores were available equaled or exceeded that score.

Table 16. Number of High-Ability Students According to Area

Area	Boys		Girls		Boys and Girls	
	1950	1961	1950	1961	1950	1961
Metropolitan	724	1,647	691	1,693	1,415	3,340
Nonfarm	867	1,225	873	1,598	1,740	2,823
Farm	315	441	469	747	784	1,188
Total	1,906	3,313	2,033	4,038	3,939	7,351

The number of high-ability students in each area is shown in Table 16. Their plans for each of the survey years are compared in Table 17. Eighty-one per cent of these students planned to attend college in 1961 as compared with 67 per cent in 1950. In college attendance a 5 percentage point increase over 1950 was found for the total 1961 graduating class.

This able group, then, with a 14 percentage point difference, has shown an increase in college attendance of almost three times that for the total group. The data indicate that the increased emphasis on the value of a college education over the past decade has had selective results as far as the ability of students who choose to attend college is

79

Table 17. Percentage Distribution of High-Ability Students According to Sex, Plan, and Area

Plan	Boys								Girls								Boys and Girls							
	Metro.		Non-farm		Farm		Total		Metro.		Non-farm		Farm		Total		Metro.		Non-farm		Farm		Total	
	'50	'61	'50	'61	'50	'61	'50	'61	'50	'61	'50	'61	'50	'61	'50	'61	'50	'61	'50	'61	'50	'61	'50	'61
Get a job	13	3	15	3	22	7	15	4	19	10	18	11	28	18	21	12	16	7	16	8	25	14	18	8
Go to college	81	90	73	88	61	82	74	88	70	81	63	75	48	61	62	75	75	85	68	81	53	69	67	81
Go to other school ..	4	2	7	3	11	3	6	2	7	4	10	6	13	10	10	6	5	3	9	4	12	8	8	4
Military service	2	5	5	6	6	8	4	6									1	3	3	3	2	3	2	3
Nursing									5	5	8	8	12	10	8	7	2	2	4	5	7	7	4	4
Total	100	100	100	100	100	100	99	100	101	100	99	100	101	99	101	100	99	100	100	101	99	101	99	100

concerned. It has not had the effect of encouraging equally all students at all levels of ability to attend college as has often been inferred.

Among the metropolitan and nonfarm high-ability boys, approximately 90 per cent planned to attend college and 2 per cent other types of schools. Of the 8 per cent seeking jobs or entering the military service, approximately half intended to go to college at a later date. Over 95 per cent of this group, then, planned on a college education.

Table 18. Percentage Distribution of Students with Different Plans in the Top Decile* on Both High School Rank and MSAT

Plan	Boys				Girls				Total
	Metro.	Non-farm	Farm	Total	Metro.	Non-farm	Farm	Total	
Get a job	0	1	2	1	4	6	11	7	4
Go to college	97	94	94	95	89	84	72	83	88
Go to other school	1	1	0	1	2	4	7	3	2
Military service	1	3	2	2					1
Nursing					3	4	8	5	3
Other	1	2	2	1	2	2	2	2	2
Total	100	101	100	100	100	100	100	100	100
N	312	308	168	788	393	437	290	1120	1908

* Top 4.5 per cent of population.

To examine further the plans of the top students, they were observed in yet another way. A sample was drawn which included all students who placed in the top decile on both MSAT and high school rank. There were 1908 such students representing the top 4.5 per cent of the graduating seniors. The plans of this group are shown in Table 18. Ninety-five per cent of the boys and 83 per cent of the girls planned to attend college. Among the metropolitan boys, the proportion of students planning to go directly on to college was particularly high — 97 per cent. Of the 312 boys in this group, 304 were planning to attend college in the fall. When the percentages of girls entering nursing are added to those planning on college, the totals approach those for the men except among the farm women, where a number of extremely able girls were not going to college.

Studies summarized by Wolfbein (1959) indicate that in many areas in the country the number of high-ability students dropping out of high school before graduation has reached negligible proportions. This study now presents evidence that the number not continuing their education beyond high school has also diminished to a relatively small percentage. Studies such as those by Iffert (1958) and Thistlethwaite (1963) have shown a high rate of attrition exists in most colleges in the country, even among relatively able students. These results suggest that emphasis on holding our young people in educational institutions until they have been trained to make the fullest use of their high potential should now be directed at the collegiate level.

These results also reveal that considerable progress needs to be made in encouraging high-ability girls from all areas and high-ability males from rural areas (and undoubtedly males from urban slum areas not present to any large degree in Minnesota) to continue their education beyond the high school level.

REFERENCES

Iffert, R. E. *Retention and Withdrawal of College Students.* U.S. Office of Education Bulletin, No. 1 (1958).

Thistlethwaite, Donald L. "Recruitment and Retention of Talented Students." Mimeographed report to Cooperative Reserve Program. Office of Education, U.S. Department of Health, Education, and Welfare (1963).

Wolfbein, S. L. "Transition from School to Work: A Study of the School Leaver." *Personnel and Guidance Journal,* 38 (1959), 98–105.

7

Effects of School and Community
on Decisions for College

DECISIONS of high school students to attend college are related to other attitudes and behavioral tendencies. These predispositions all are formed by the many experiences which constitute the student's life. These experiences in turn are influenced by families, teachers, friends, geography, finances, and other facts in the student's behavioral history.

Most of the determinants of post-high-school plans reported in this study prior to this chapter have been inferred from the student's comments about himself and his background. With the exception of test scores and high school percentile rank, all the variables have been obtained from a questionnaire eliciting verbal responses from the student. Students' plans are related to what they have to say about their socioeconomic status, to the number of books they report in their homes, and to similar self-statements. Major attention has been given to characteristics of the student and his immediate family.

Examination of the questionnaires revealed that the percentage of students planning to attend college varied not only from area to area but also from high school to high school. In some schools 5 per cent of the graduates were planning to attend college; in other schools all of them were. Table 19 shows the distribution of schools according to the percentage planning to attend college for 1950 and 1961.

Considerable variation is found among schools not only in the percentage planning to attend college but also in socioeconomic status and ability of students. One would expect that schools with the highest percentages of high-ability students, as shown by scores on college aptitude

Table 19. Number and Percentage of Schools with Varying
Proportions of Seniors Planning to Attend College
in 1950 and 1961

Percentage of Seniors Planning to Attend College	Number of Schools		Percentage of Schools	
	1950*	1961†	1950*	1961†
100	5	1	1	0
95–99	2	4	0	1
90–94	1	6	0	1
85–89	3	2	1	0
80–84	2	3	0	1
75–79	3	5	1	1
70–74	2	9	0	2
65–69	5	4	1	1
60–64	7	4	1	1
55–59	6	13	1	2
50–54	17	22	3	4
45–49	18	32	4	6
40–44	35	66	7	12
35–39	49	83	10	15
30–34	63	84	13	15
25–29	94	84	19	15
20–24	78	65	16	12
15–19	53	38	11	7
10–14	28	17	6	3
5–9	18	5	4	1
0–4	7	0	1	0

* N = 496.
† N = 547.

tests, would have more students planning to attend college than those with the lowest. Similarly, if one took schools with many students from upper socioeconomic homes, one would expect to find more students planning to attend college than in schools where many came from lower socioeconomic homes. Comparison of college attendance rates of schools divided according to various characteristics related to college attendance would not reveal much about the influence of the school and the community on decisions to attend college.

A more indirect method of observation was employed here. The authors hypothesized that if school and community influences were important to decisions, schools showing changes over a decade in percentage of students planning to attend college should also show other changes. Where this percentage increased, accompanying changes could be the development of counseling programs, the introduction of honors programs, the improvement of teachers and instruction, and the expansion of co-curricular activities. One also might hypothesize that schools with increasing percentages going on to college were affected by changes in the community or were drawing students from different kinds of

Table 20. Schools Showing an Increase in Percentage of Seniors Planning on College in 1961, in Contrast to 1950, in the School-Community Characteristics Study

Code	1950	1961	Code	1950	1961
*Small Schools**			678	11	32
			742	12	37
202	6	39	858	26	47
205	0	31	880	18	41
270	14	50	884	17	43
288	25	67	016X	26	43
474	31	70	120	20	38
496	33	72	464	7	27
584	4	40	500	20	39
646	14	50	164Y	15	33
768	0	43	568	19	38
864	0	31	150Y	13	32
402	6	36	638	15	34
572	10	39	770	24	44
780	13	40			
784	19	75	*Large Schools‡*		
			228	28	44
Medium Schools†			320	25	42
002	15	46	448	25	57
104	27	63	546	33	37
192	19	46	712	25	41
274	13	25	764	25	44
302	39	58	772	29	48
316	20	42	154Y	27	50
354	18	49	172Y	39	57
504	14	42	142Y	54	78
544	13	34	122Y	56	22
600	24	48			
664	12	34			

* Median increase, 36 per cent.
† Median increase, 21 per cent.
‡ Median increase, 19 per cent.

communities. New housing areas could be attracting large numbers of upper-middle-class residents to the school district; average pupil expenditures could be increasing; and new colleges in neighboring areas could also be an influential factor.

For this analysis, schools first were divided into three groups according to size of senior class. The small-school group was composed of schools having 30 or fewer seniors; the medium-size group, between 31 and 100 seniors; and the large-school group, more than 100 seniors.

Table 21. Schools Showing a Decrease in Percentage of Seniors Planning on College in 1961, in Contrast to 1950, in the School-Community Characteristics Study

Code	1950	1961	Code	1950	1961
Small Schools *			420 60		37
168 54		17	444 27		15
222 33		14	468 36		27
284 38		16	488 37		22
342 50		25	574 36		25
418 45		25	608 19		11
484 42		13	618 40		19
656 43		22	676 50		15
756 23		9	698 52		42
758 42		12	726 60		35
796 45		19	776 31		21
896 50		28	906 41		19
956 38		25	922 36		24
132Y 44		29	982 42		26
180Y 75		17	160Y 100		98
Medium Schools†			*Large Schools*‡		
004 40		29	160 53		24
134 35		26	330 31		19
144 28		18	748 28		18
146 30		20	750 44		31
170 22		21	812 46		31
178 35		26	958 65		45
182 53		25	966 63		50
278 65		32	011X 66		39
362 33		24	041X 70		59
386 42		25	115Y 48		37
			170Y 62		41

* Median decrease, 22 per cent.
† Median decrease, 11 per cent.
‡ Median decrease, 13 per cent.

Within each group the 10 per cent of the schools showing the largest and the 10 per cent showing the smallest percentage increase in seniors planning on college were selected for study. In most cases the schools in the latter group showed an actual decrease in percentage of college-bound seniors.

Tables 20 and 21 list by code number the schools included in the six subsamples and show the percentage of students planning to attend college in 1950 and 1961.

To each school a list of questions entitled "Trends in Post-High-School Plans School Questionnaire" was sent after a letter requesting cooperation had been forwarded to the superintendent of the school system. Intensive follow-up resulted in questionnaires being returned from 13 of the 14 small schools showing increases in percentages, 13 of the 14 small schools showing decreases in percentages, 24 of the 25 medium size schools showing increases in percentages, 23 of the 25 medium schools showing decreases in percentages, 10 of the 11 large schools showing increases in percentages, and 10 of the 11 large schools showing decreases in percentages. Thus returns were obtained from 93 per cent of the schools. Complete data were not available for each of the schools since many schools omitted answers to one or more questions.

The questionnaire was designed to provide information on the following topics:

number of school days in school year

number of class periods spent in school by each student

total number of students in grades 9 through 12

average instructional class size

average amount of daily homework for students in grade 11

number of study halls per week for average student in grades 9 through 12

special classes provided

accelerated curriculums

advanced placement provided

meaning of grades in subject

types of course grades given

principal basis for assigning pupils to classes

summer school

religious education provided

participation in inter-system try-out of special experimental curriculum

school developed special experimental curriculum

average daily percentage of absenteeism

tenure situation

need for additional staff

number of books in the library

extracurricular activities

average number of years of experience of teachers

percentage of all boys entering 10th grade who drop out before graduation excluding transfers

percentage of all girls who drop out

percentage of students with one or both parents in PTA

frequency of PTA meetings

primary type of residence served by school

description of area from which students come

average per pupil expenditure

current school tax rate per $1000 evaluation

percentages of students coming from homes where one or more foreign languages are regularly spoken

number of elementary schools in system

school consolidation affecting school

employers coming into community

employers leaving community

guidance program with one or more full-time counselors

number of persons in full-time guidance positions

number of part-time guidance counselors

homogeneous grouping of students by ability

acceleration policy

policy on retarding slow learners

number of full-time classroom teachers

percentage of men teachers

number of teachers with master's degrees

number of teachers with graduate training in area they teach

number of teachers attending summer school the previous summer

number of teachers attending summer institutes sponsored by the government or other national organizations

annual starting salaries for male teachers with bachelor degrees and no experience.

starting salaries for female teachers with bachelor degrees and no experience

amount of time devoted to guidance in terms of minutes per week devoted to students

number of guidance personnel of each sex

counselors' experience, background, and qualifications

length of time school has had to organize guidance program

kinds of tests given

grades at which tests are given

guidance materials available for student use

adequacy of guidance facilities

adequacy of referral sources in community

conditions under which conferences are held with parents

changes in counseling program

In many instances the school was asked to provide information on school or community characteristic as of 1950 and as of 1961. The retrospective data are of unknown validity since the school personnel reporting the information was not always the same as in 1950, and even when respondents had been at the school for the eleven years, their records or memories often were not adequate to providing a good picture of the school as it was eleven years ago. To win the cooperation of the principals who had primary responsibility for completing the questionnaire they were instructed, "Please do not spend a great deal of time in searching for precise answers; however, we would appreciate your providing the best estimates you can based on information readily available to you."

We can assume that the data descriptive of the schools for 1961 are reasonably accurate. No such assumption can be made about the descriptions of school or community conditions in 1950, and to this unknown extent any failure to support the hypotheses studied here may be due to the inadequacies of the early data.

DIFFERENCES AMONG SCHOOLS

In general the comparisons between schools showing decreasing and increasing proportions of college planners brought out some differences.

Changes in the number of books in the school library offer a case in point. Superficially, the size of the library is an index of academic quality. We hypothesized that schools characterized by increasing numbers of graduates attending college also would have increased the size of the library to a greater extent than schools with corresponding decreases. The number of books in libraries in 1950 and 1961 for the two groups of schools is shown in Table 22. Of schools with a decrease in number of college planners, 9 out of 39 had fewer than 1000 books in 1950; all 43 reporting in 1961 had more than 1000 books. Of schools with an increase in number of college planners, 7 out of 45 in 1950 had fewer than 1000 books; all 46 reporting in 1961 had more than 1000 books. Combining categories provides the distribution of percentages shown at the bottom of Table 22.

Of the "decrease" schools, about three fourths in 1950 had fewer than 2500 library books; in 1961 about the same proportion had more than 2500. Of the "increase" schools, about one half had fewer than 2500 in 1950; in 1961, about one fifth. Both groups improved markedly in this respect, and in terms of percentage points the decrease schools improved most. One cannot assume, however, that an increase of from 26 to 72 per cent is greater than an increase of from 47 to 80 per cent, because the larger the initial percentage the more difficult it may be to achieve each increment of improvement. In this instance both groups of schools increased the size of their school libraries.

Table 22. Size of Library in Schools Showing Decrease and Increase in Percentage of Graduates Planning to Attend College

No. of Books	Schools with Decrease		Schools with Increase	
	1950	1961	1950	1961
Number of Schools				
Less than 500	3	0	4	0
500–999	6	0	3	0
1000–1499	5	3	5	2
1500–1999	7	5	5	2
2000–2499	8	4	7	5
More than 2500	10	31	21	37
Total	39	43	45	46
Percentage Distribution of Schools				
Less than 2499	74%	28%	53%	20%
More than 2500	26%	72%	47%	80%

89

Noteworthy is the fact here that the increase group was superior to the decrease group in both 1950 and 1961, and that this superiority was especially noticeable in 1950. Almost one half of the former group in 1950 had more than 2500 books, as compared with only slightly more than one fourth of the latter group. During the eleven-year interval, the decrease group tended to catch up, but size of school library may be a cause or an expression of a more subtle school atmosphere that affects students and faculty slowly and in complex ways over a long period of time.

Table 23 presents data on size of school library for small, medium, and large schools. Of the ten large schools with a decrease in college planners, only five in 1950 had more than 2500 books, whereas by 1961 all did. Among the ten large schools with an increase in college planners, nine had this number of books in 1950 and all in 1961.

Table 23. Size of Library in Small, Medium, and Large Schools Showing Decrease and Increase in Percentage of Graduates Planning to Attend College

| | No. of "Decrease" Schools | | | | | | No. of "Increase" Schools | | | | | |
| | Small | | Medium | | Large | | Small | | Medium | | Large | |
No. of Books	'50	'61	'50	'61	'50	'61	'50	'61	'50	'61	'50	'61
Less than 500	2	0	1	0	0	0	4	0	0	0	0	0
500–999	2	0	4	0	0	0	1	0	2	0	0	0
1000–1499	1	2	4	1	0	0	2	1	3	1	0	0
1500–1999	2	2	3	3	2	0	2	2	2	0	1	0
2000–2499	2	1	3	3	3	0	2	3	5	2	0	0
More than 2500	1	6	4	15	5	10	2	7	10	20	9	10

The remaining information from the analysis of questionnaires returned by the schools will be summarized in less detail. The decrease schools reported a median of 170 days in the school year in 1950 and 173 in 1961. The increase medians were 172 and 175. Both groups lengthened their school year by three days during the eleven-year interval and in both years the increase group had a longer median school year.

The average number of class periods each day spent in school by each student for the decrease group was 5.85 in 1950, 6.39 in 1961. For the increase group, the means were 6.0 and 6.30. The increase group had slightly more class periods in 1950; the decrease group more than caught up.

The increase group had slightly greater mean numbers of students in both 1950 and 1961, 185 and 233 in grades nine through twelve, as compared with 150 and 207 for the decrease group. The increase group reported smaller average instructional class sizes than the decrease group, but the averages for the two groups did not change during the eleven years. The two groups did not differ in either year on amount of daily homework required or on number of study hall periods per week per average student.

The increase and decrease groups differed on special academic programs. In 1950, among 20 decrease schools, a total of 23 special classes was reported. Among 29 increase schools, the total was 39. In 1961 the total for 40 decrease schools was 84 and for 46 increase schools, 110. The increase schools had more special classes in 1950 and proportionately more in 1961.

Among 45 decrease schools, a total of 33 accelerated curriculums was reported in 1961, as compared with 45 among 47 increase schools. Slightly more of the latter group had such programs. Although relatively few schools in 1961 provided opportunity for advanced placement work in high school, 5 per cent of the decrease group and 17 per cent of the increase group did.

The groups did not appear to differ on how they used school marks or grading methods.

In the decrease group, 9 per cent reported summer classes in 1961 as compared with 21 per cent of the increase group. Less than 6 per cent in either group reported summer programs in 1950.

The schools varied in their responses to the question on religious instruction. Responses to this item are presented in the accompanying tabulation. Neither group changed much from year to year, but the increase group during both years had more religion in the curriculums and included more schools with no religious education.

	No. of "Decrease" Schools		No. of "Increase" Schools	
	1950	1961	1950	1961
Included in regular curriculum	4	4	7	6
Released time for all	24	28	17	20
Released time for some	8	6	4	7
None	6	7	19	15

91

The increase group in 1961 tended to experiment with new curriculums more than the decrease group, but differences were small and inconsistent. Few differences between groups were found regarding absenteeism or teacher tenure (67 of 90 schools reported no tenure in 1961; 62 of 86 reported none in 1950). The groups did not differ on expressed need for additional professional staff, although 33 per cent of the decrease group and only 13 per cent of the increase group expressed a need for additional maintenance workers. Sixty of the 93 schools expressed a need for more counselors, 38 for more teachers, 35 for more clerical staff, and 28 for more administrative and supervisory staff.

Some differences were observed between the increase and decrease groups on the basis of extracurricular activities. In most instances more increase than decrease schools reported specific activities in both 1950 and 1961. Differences between the two groups were greater in 1950; of the 45 decrease schools reporting, 4 had National Honor Societies in 1950 as compared with 21 of the 47 increase schools. In 1961 the figures were 8 and 25. The proportion in the decrease group had doubled; in the increase group it had grown by about one fifth. In the increase group, the number reporting interschool athletics for boys had grown from 42 in 1950 to 45 in 1961; in the decrease group it had dropped from 39 to 34. The figures for extracurricular activities are shown in Table 24.

The average decrease school reported 7.53 activities in 1950 and 10.96 in 1961, and the average increase school, 8.49 and 11.38.

Both in 1950 and 1961 more increase than decrease groups reported homogeneous grouping by ability, summer acceleration programs, and required repetition of courses for needed credits. In 1961 the increase group had more teachers, about the same proportion of men teachers, and slightly more teachers with master's degrees than the other group.

None of the schools reported male starting salaries of $4500 or over in 1950, whereas in the increase group 16 (36 per cent) of 45 schools and in the decrease group 11 of the 44 schools (25 per cent) reported these salaries in 1961. Similar differences were reported for beginning salaries for women.

The increase and decrease groups did not differ on reported dropout rates in 1961, the average between grade ten and graduation being less than 10 per cent.

Table 24. Number of Schools with Decreasing or Increasing Percentage of
Graduates Planning to Attend College and Reporting
Extracurricular Activities

Activity	"Decrease" Schools		"Increase" Schools	
	1950	1961	1950	1961
Student government	27	41	30	41
Newspaper	39	44	42	45
Magazine, annual	37	33	39	44
Inter-school athletics				
Boys	39	34	42	45
Girls	4	5	2	4
Intramural athletics				
Boys	17	28	22	31
Girls	15	26	17	27
Orchestra, band	36	43	40	45
Glee club	36	43	43	45
Fraternities, sororities	1	0	1	1
National Honor Society	4	8	21	25
Subject clubs	9	32	15	39
Chess clubs	2	4	1	7
Hobby clubs	3	7	4	8
Drama	39	45	43	46
Debate	7	17	8	15
Dances	20	42	30	39
Service clubs	2	13	5	12
Other	0	0	2	7
Religious	2	6	5	9
Total activities	339	504	399	535
Mean activities	7.53	10.96	8.49	11.38
Number of schools	45	46	47	47

In the decrease group, the average school reported 19 per cent of its students had one or both parents in the PTA, whereas in the increase group, this average was 28 per cent. The increase group also reported more frequent PTA meetings.

No consistent differences were reported between the two groups in either year on the primary type of residents served by the school except that both in 1950 and 1961, 11 of the 38 reporting decrease schools said they served prosperous farm areas, as compared with 6 of the 34 increase schools reporting for 1950 and 6 of the 32 reporting for 1961. Slightly more of the increase group in both years described their area as one of "moderate priced homes." More of the decrease schools drew pupils primarily from farm areas in both years. Differential changes were not reported.

The two groups did not differ on reported average expenditure per student or school tax rate in either 1950 or 1961.

The decrease schools listed 55 employers as entering the communities during the decade and 35 as leaving, the increase schools 47 coming and 33 leaving. A slight trend appeared here for more employers to enter areas served by the large schools with fewer college planners — 42 reported by eight large decrease schools as compared to 19 reported by ten large increase schools. Perhaps more employment opportunities developed in the former areas.

The increase and decrease groups did not differ in proportions having guidance programs. In 1950, 26 per cent of the decrease and 22 per cent of the increase schools, and in 1961, 83 per cent of each group had guidance programs with one or more full-time counselors. In 1961 the increase group reported an average of .83 full-time guidance persons per school, the decrease group an average of .67. The increase group reported 5.3 minutes per day of guidance time per pupil, the decrease group 3.9 minutes. The counselors in the increase group were reported as far better qualified than those in the decrease group. In the forty-seven increase schools, 60 counselors had completed practicum training, as compared with 32 in the forty-six decrease schools. In general the increase schools reported older and more extensive guidance programs than the decrease schools. They tended to use more tests, particularly in 1950. The two groups did not differ as much in 1961 as in 1950, the decrease schools having caught up in many ways with the increase schools.

In summary, the analysis of the questionnaire responses from the schools failed to substantiate the original hypothesis. Schools with more college planners in 1961 than in 1950 had not improved markedly more or undergone greater community changes than schools with fewer college planners in 1961 than in 1950. Some trends were found of the differential changes that were hypothesized, but these appeared unimportant in the light of more obvious findings.

Both groups of schools had changed their programs greatly during the eleven years. New programs were developed, more money was spent, salaries were increased, and academic emphasis was increased. The over-all improvements reported by both groups of schools were so great that differences in amounts of improvement between groups of schools were hard to detect. To an unknown extent this is influenced by the questionable accuracy of retrospective reports such as were used here.

Perhaps the most significant conclusion from this analysis derives from the reportedly higher status in 1950 of the schools with increasing proportions of college planners. Almost every comparison showed that in 1950 those schools had more programs, better salaries, more money, and better facilities than the others. Both groups improved. The decrease group started from a lower level in 1950. The increase group was striving to improve when it already was at a level where each increment of improvement may have been more difficult to achieve. These schools were better schools in 1950; during the decade their superiority as a group was reduced. This, in a sense, suggests the research design employed was not appropriate. Ideally, increase and decrease schools should have been matched on the proportion of college-planning students in 1950.

REPORTED CHANGES

Changes in the two groups of schools discussed in this chapter have been inferred on the basis of comparisons of conditions in 1950 and 1961 as reported by the schools. One of the last sections in the questionnaire gave the schools an opportunity to check specific changes in their counseling programs that occurred during the decade. The responses of the two groups are shown in Table 25.

The forty-six reporting schools with decreasing proportions of college planners checked a total of 524 improvements (not including the three items implying retrenchment), or an average of 11.4 items per school. The forty-seven increase schools reported 561 items, or an average of 11.9 per school. These gross figures suggest substantial improvements in both groups of schools, but if the increase group improved more than the decrease group the difference was not great.

Five more increase than decrease schools reported additional full-time counselors, more personal contact with parents, and more follow-up work. Seven more indicated greater participation in national testing programs.

Almost all the schools reported increases in contacts with parents and students, testing, national and state-wide testing programs, personnel and cumulative records, and use of test results.

95

Table 25. Number of Schools in the Decrease and Increase Groups
Reporting Changes in Counseling Programs between 1950 and 1961

Change	Decrease Group (N = 46)	Increase Group (N = 47)
More full-time counselors	12	17
Fewer full-time counselors	2	1
More part-time counselors	22	22
Fewer part-time counselors	3	2
Training for counselors	29	30
More clerks	15	17
More personal contact with students	38	42
More personal contact with parents	35	40
More follow-up work	30	35
More standardized tests	41	41
Fewer standardized tests	2	1
National testing program	35	42
State or regional testing program	41	42
More detailed personnel records	43	44
Fewer detailed personnel records	0	0
Better use of test results	40	43
Cumulative records	43	44
More referral services available	34	34
Research	24	25
Minnesota state-wide testing program	42	42
Other	0	1

These "self-reports" indicate a great improvement in both quality and quantity of counseling programs in these two samples of schools during the decade. The similarity of the responses from the two samples suggests that the reported developments from the 93 schools present a reasonably representative picture of what such reports would be from all Minnesota schools. The validity or accuracy of these reports, however, is another question.

The implication is clear. If schools wish to alter their programs in order to influence more graduates (presumably qualified) to continue their educations, such changes will require time in which to achieve the desired effect. Post-high-school plans of students are closely related to what can be called school atmosphere, which is a result of many interacting conditions in the school and the community. Specific improvements in program slowly and subtly influence school atmosphere, and only after sufficient time has elapsed to permit development of the proper atmosphere will plans of students begin to reflect these changes, with more graduates in subsequent years deciding to go to college.

· 8

Personal Values and Attitudes

FOR students in 1950 and 1961, post-high-school plans were related to ability, sex, academic record, socioeconomic status, and the region from which they came. Within any one group, however homogeneous on the basis of these variables, students differed in choice of plan. A group restricted to those with high test scores, superior school grades, and families with similar educational and economic backgrounds included some who planned to attend college and others who planned to seek employment immediately after graduation from high school. Although much of the variance explaining post-high-school plans can be attributed to these variables, much of the source of variance remains to be identified.

An attempt was made to explore some of the more obscure determinants of post-high-school plans by investigating the social and personal attitudes, values, and experiences of students. The attitudes elicited by the questionnaire were directly related to social behavior and social conformity. An attempt was made to study how students who decide to attend college were different from others on the basis of these personality variables.

The questionnaire contained 25 personality inventory items from the Minnesota Counseling Inventory (MCI). Thirteen of these items were the most discriminating of all 61 items from the social relations scale and twelve were the most discriminating of all 35 items from the conformity scale. Scores on the social relations scale refer to the nature of the student's relations with other people. Students with low scores are generally gregarious and appear to be happy and comfortable with

Table 26. Percentage of Seniors Responding "True" to Questionnaire Statements*

Statement	Boys Metro. Job	Boys Metro. Col.	Boys Nonfarm Job	Boys Nonfarm Col.	Boys Farm Job	Boys Farm Col.	Girls Metro. Job	Girls Metro. Col.	Girls Nonfarm Job	Girls Nonfarm Col.	Girls Farm Job	Girls Farm Col.
1. I meet strangers easily. (SR)	68	76	68	76	64	71	65	77	68	78	66	72
2. I get along as well as the average person in social activities. (SR)	88	94	88	94	90	94	93	97	92	97	92	95
3. In school I sometimes have been sent to the principal for cutting up. (C)	41	23	43	28	38	23	10	6	10	6	7	5
4. I feel self-conscious when reciting in class. (SR)	62	45	64	44	64	52	73	49	71	48	73	50
5. I am sure I get a raw deal from life. (C)	9	3	10	3	10	3	3	4	5	2	5	1
6. I feel at ease with people. (SR)	69	80	67	81	71	77	76	84	72	83	72	79
7. At times I have very much wanted to leave home. (C)	50	31	49	30	47	27	51	35	51	34	43	29
8. I have difficulty in starting a conversation with a person who has just been introduced. (SR)	50	36	51	37	56	47	41	29	44	31	49	39
9. I find it hard to keep my mind on a task or job. (C)	25	23	21	23	18	20	21	22	24	22	23	19
10. I enjoy speaking before groups of people. (SR)	11	29	8	26	9	22	11	29	10	29	9	28
11. I know who is responsible for most of my troubles. (C)	60	63	59	64	60	60	68	70	66	73	60	67
12. My parents have often objected to the kind of people I go around with. (C)	30	12	32	13	25	11	20	8	24	8	20	6
13. I am rather shy in contacts with people. (SR)	35	27	39	27	42	36	38	29	39	29	46	37
14. No one seems to understand me. (C)	14	8	13	9	13	9	12	8	14	9	12	10
15. I enjoy entertaining people. (SR)	51	65	46	61	41	53	70	77	64	72	64	66
16. My family does not like the work I have chosen or the work I intend to choose for my life work. (C)	11	3	9	2	8	3	5	4	5	4	4	3
17. I like to meet new people. (SR)	83	89	82	87	82	86	90	94	91	94	92	92
18. My parents and family find more fault with me than they should. (C)	25	14	23	14	19	14	18	10	18	11	17	10
19. I dislike social affairs. (SR)	24	10	29	13	20	12	9	4	10	6	9	7

* Significant differences (.05 level) are listed in the text.

Table 26 — Continued

	Boys						Girls					
	Metro.		Nonfarm		Farm		Metro.		Nonfarm		Farm	
Statement	Job	Col.	Job	Col.	Job	Col.	Job	Col.	Job	Col.	Job	Col.
20. If people had not had it in for me I would have been much more successful. (C)	5	2	7	2	6	2	3	1	3	1	3	1
21. I find it easy to express my ideas. (SR)	43	58	41	59	38	51	38	51	36	53	35	48
22. I wish I were not so shy. (C)	44	33	44	34	52	45	44	33	43	33	51	42
23. I avoid people when it is possible. (SR)	19	11	21	11	18	13	12	6	13	6	12	9
24. I have had very peculiar and strange experiences. (C)	42	32	43	34	41	31	35	25	35	30	31	23
25. I stay in the background at parties or social gatherings. (SR)	26	21	29	21	29	24	17	16	19	15	35	23
26. Most of my close friends are planning to go to college.	38	86	37	86	26	77	35	85	33	84	27	73
27. Would you say that your high school grades are a fairly accurate reflection of your ability? (Yes response) ..	34	41	34	43	40	54	57	62	59	65	68	76
28. Do you think that most of the important things that happen to people are:												
More the result of circumstances beyond their control.	10	5	10	4	11	5	6	3	7	3	7	5
More the result of their own efforts.	85	94	88	95	87	94	92	96	92	96	92	95
29. If you had your choice, which type of job would you pick?												
(a) A job which pays quite a low income but which you are sure of keeping.	27	13	29	15	29	18	41	24	44	28	46	32
(b) A job which pays a good income but which you have a 50/50 chance of losing.	39	39	43	43	48	48	41	48	40	47	42	50
(c) A job which pays an extremely good income if you make the grade, but in which you lose almost everything if you don't make it.	31	44	26	40	21	33	16	26	14	23	10	17
N	970	4,414	1,204	3,753	1,239	1,670	2,391	3,655	2,430	3,151	2,421	1,490

others. Usually they have well-developed social skills. Students with high scores tend to be socially inept and unhappy, and uncomfortable in their relations with peers and adults. The conformity scale was derived from the psychopathic deviate scale of the Minnesota Multiphasic Personality Inventory (MMPI). Students with low scores usually are reliable and responsible. Although not necessarily docile or overly submissive, they understand the need for behavior codes and social organization. Students with high scores are likely to be irresponsible, impulsive, and rebellious. They tend to be individualistic and self-centered, and some have juvenile court records. In addition to items from these two scales, four other items were included which dealt with willingness to take risks and willingness to accept responsibility for one's behavior.

Responses to these personality items by seniors who planned to get a job following high school graduation were compared with the responses of seniors who planned to attend college. Separate analyses were done for the sexes and for each of the three residence-area groups — metropolitan, farm, and nonfarm. Responses to these items are shown according to sex, area, and plan in Table 26.

SEX DIFFERENCES

The two sexes responded differently to many of the items. Significant differences (.05 level) were found on nine of the thirteen social relations items (2, 4, 6, 8, 15, 17, 19, 23, 25), with girls responding more often in the direction of better social relations. Boys showed significantly less conformity on seven of the twelve items from the conformity scale (3, 5, 11, 12, 18, 20, 24). In general, girls responded to statements in a way that indicated they were more sociable than boys, and the boys' responses suggested that they were more often in trouble with their families or with other authority figures.

More girls than boys felt that their high school grades were an accurate reflection of their ability. On the item dealing with willingness to risk taking an insecure but extremely well-paid job, girls were more conservative than boys. Among the metropolitan girls planning to attend college, 26 per cent were willing to take a job that provided a very good income but which they might easily lose, whereas 44 per cent of the college-bound metropolitan boys were willing to take this risk.

DIFFERENCES BETWEEN GEOGRAPHIC REGIONS

In their responses to these items, the boys and girls from the metropolitan areas and from the nonfarm areas were remarkably similar. Comparisons of the farm students with those from the other two areas, however, revealed greater differences. For the boys, significant differences were found between the other two groups and the farm group on seven social relations items (1, 4, 8, 13, 15, 21, 22) and three conformity items (3, 9, 12). Among the girls significant differences were also found on seven social relations items (1, 6, 8, 13, 15, 22, 25) and three conformity items (7, 11, 24). These differences in responses showed that boys and girls from the farm had less social confidence and perhaps felt less need for social behavior than the other students. Of the metropolitan boys planning to attend college, 45 per cent reported feeling self-conscious when reciting in class, compared with 52 per cent of the farm boys with similar plans. Thirty-six per cent of the metropolitan college-bound boys, and 47 per cent of the boys from the farm, said they had difficulty in starting a conversation with a person who has just been introduced. Exactly one third of the metropolitan college-planning boys said they wished they were not so shy, a response checked by almost half the farm boys.

More difficult to interpret is the difference in response between these two groups on the item "Would you say that your high school grades are a fairly accurate reflection of your ability?" Significantly more farm boys agreed with this statement. Significantly more farm boys expressed a preference for a fair income with a fairly safe job, whereas more metropolitan boys were willing to gamble on a good income in a job that was less safe. In general, the differences were in the same direction and of a comparable size for the girls.

The items showing the greatest differences among the regional groups were those from the social relations scale of the MCI. There is little question that young people coming from the farm differ from other students in social skills and attitudes.

DIFFERENCES AMONG STUDENTS WITH VARYING PLANS

Although metropolitan, nonfarm, and farm students varied in their responses to many of the items, the differences between college- and job-planning students tended to remain constant from one region to the other. Therefore only the metropolitan groups will be discussed here, as these differences apply equally well for the other areas.

Among metropolitan boys, when those planning to get jobs were compared with those planning to attend college, differences were statistically significant beyond the .01 level of probability for all items from the social relations scale and for all but two of the items from the conformity scale (9 and 11). Responses were significantly different for all but one (29b) of the non-MCI items.

Because of the large number of cases involved in these comparisons, 970 job-seeking and 4414 college-planning men, a small difference in proportions attains statistical significance. Examination of the figures reveals that these differences are more than just statistically significant, that they have many practical applications.

In each case, the students contemplating college saw themselves as being more sociable, expressed less shyness, and had fewer conflicts with family and authorities. Not only did these two groups differ in socioeconomic status and abilities, but also in social experiences and attitudes.

Some of the differences were quite large. Twenty-nine per cent of the college-planning students said they enjoyed speaking before groups of people, as compared with 11 per cent of the boys planning on jobs. Related to this is a difference in response to the item "I feel self-conscious when reciting in class." Of college-planning boys, 45 per cent expressed self-consciousness; of the job-seeking boys, 62 per cent. In both groups a large proportion of students expressed social satisfaction. Although more college-planning than job-planning students said they enjoyed meeting new people, even among the job-planning group 83 per cent responded affirmatively to this item. The large majority of job seekers expressed no dislike for social affairs, although the difference between the two groups here was great, with 24 per cent of the job seekers and only 10 per cent of the college planners disliking social affairs.

The differences were even larger for the conformity items. Close to one half of the job seekers, 41 per cent, had been sent to the principal for discipline, as compared with 23 per cent of the college planners. One half of the job seekers, but less than one third of the college planners, at one time or another had very much wanted to leave home. More than twice as many job seekers as college planners reported their

102

parents had objected to their friends. Apparently most of these students had chosen work of which their families approved, although 11 per cent of the job planners reported family disapproval of their occupational plans, as compared with only 3 per cent of the college planners. The two groups differed significantly in responses to how accurately their school grades reflected their ability. More college planners regarded their school grades as an accurate reflection of their ability, although only 41 per cent (as compared with 34 per cent of the job seekers) agreed with this statement. Whether disagreement implied that the student regarded his school grades as an over- or an under-reflection of his performance is not known.

One of the most interesting and significant differences concerned the willingness of the two groups to take risks on jobs. The proportions expressing a preference for a job which pays a good income and offers moderate security were the same, but twice as many job seekers preferred a low-income, secure job, and 44 per cent of the college planners preferred a high-income, less secure job as compared with only 31 per cent of the job seekers. Obviously these boys were not a security-ridden group, although a significant proportion of both job seekers and college planners placed much emphasis on keeping a job.

Similar comparisons were made between the girls from metropolitan areas who planned to get jobs and those who planned on college. For the girls the differences were statistically significant beyond the .01 level for all but one of the items (25) from the social relations scale, and for all but three of the items (9, 11, 16) from the conformity scale. Responses were significantly different for all the non-MCI items. Again the differences were impressively large.

DIFFERENCES AMONG HOMOGENEOUS GROUPS

The plans of students together with their attitudes and values vary according to their abilities and socioeconomic status. The marked relationship found between values and attitudes and post-high-school plans might be attributed to either or both of the other two variables. Therefore the data were further analyzed to determine the extent to which this was true.

A group was selected consisting of 780 boys and 1074 girls with Minnesota Scholastic Aptitude Test scores of above 45 (eighty-third

103

percentile for high school seniors) and who had fathers in occupations classified as skilled tradesmen, factory workers, laborers, or unskilled laborers. This group, then, included students falling in the upper 17 per cent of Minnesota high school graduates on the basis of college aptitude, and coming from the lower socioeconomic strata. Of the boys, 84 per cent planned to attend college; of the girls, 64 per cent. Only 6 per cent of the boys, but 16 per cent of the girls, planned to seek jobs immediately after high school. The remaining students planned to attend other kinds of schools, to join the military service, to marry, and so forth.

Responses to nine of the personality inventory items (1, 2, 3, 6, 7, 16, 19, 21, 22) were significantly different at the .05 level of probability when boys planning to attend college were compared with boys planning to get jobs; the same number of items, but different ones (6, 7, 8, 10, 12, 14, 15, 16, 18), differentiated among the girls. As reported above, for the total group 23 of the 25 items among the boys and 21 among the girls produced differences that were statistically significant. It can be assumed that some differences on many of the items are attributable to ability and socioeconomic status as related to post-high-school plans. For these nine items for each sex, however, large and statistically significant differences were found to persist between students planning on college and those planning on jobs even after attempts had been made to control the effects of both ability and socioeconomic status. In some cases the size of the difference was larger for the more homogeneous group than for the total group.

For example, in responding to the item "I meet strangers easily," the total group of metropolitan boys saying "Yes" was 68 per cent among the job-planning and 76 per cent among the college-planning contingents. Among the homogeneous ability and socioeconomic groups, the percentages were 55 and 72. The item "I get along as well as the average person in social activities" was responded to affirmatively among the total group by 88 per cent of the job-planning boys and 94 per cent of the college-planning boys. Among the more homogeneous group, 77 per cent said "Yes" among the job-planning and 92 per cent among the college-planning boys. No differences were found on the last two items pertaining to responsibility for actions and to job security.

SUMMARY

This analysis investigated the relationship between certain personality factors and students' post-high-school plans. Responses to personality inventory items varied according to the sex of the student, the region from which he came, and whether he planned to attend college.

Girls perceived themselves as being more sociable than boys did. Boys indicated more often than girls that they were in trouble with their families and other authority figures. Young people from farms appeared to be less sociable than other young people. Both boys and girls planning to attend college indicated greater social needs and more social competence than the students planning to seek jobs. College-planning students also described themselves more often as "good boys and girls" than the other students, although in any case the results provided a picture of a large group of students, regardless of plans, who considered themselves socially competent and well behaved.

A group of bright students from somewhat similar family and home backgrounds was selected and divided between those planning to attend college and those not. Again these two groups differed markedly in their responses to personality inventory items. Again the college-bound students expressed more ease in social situations, less difficulty with authority figures, and more favorable relationships with the family. These attitudes and personal values continued to differentiate between students who planned to attend college and those who planned to seek jobs after graduation from high school even in this homogeneous group.

9

Socioeconomic and Ability Variables

ONE method of examining the relationships between social and psychological variables and college attendance is to compute correlation coefficients between these variables and post-high-school plans. Since similar data were available for both 1950 and 1961 students, correlations could be computed in order to study changes in relationships which occurred over the intervening eleven years. In this way a number of questions could be answered: Has ability become more, or less, important as a determinant of college attendance? Have socioeconomic variables become more, or less, important? Has income alone become a more, or less, important determinant? How have changes in the relationship between college attendance and socioeconomic status compared with similar changes in that between college attendance and ability and achievement?

The total sample of seniors was divided according to sex and residence area. From these groups random samples were selected consisting of students who planned to attend college and those who planned to get jobs, and for whom complete socioeconomic and ability data were available. Each of the socioeconomic and ability variables was correlated with the dichotomous variable of college-employment. Students with other plans were excluded from this analysis.

Pearson product-moment correlations were used, this being the only technique available in a computer program for multiple correlations. Although certain of the assumptions based on correlation coefficients may not hold for situations where one of the variables is dichotomous, it is still useful to compare results when all correlations have been calculated by the same method.

106

In computing correlations, the variable "planning to attend college" was assigned to the highest integer. Therefore, for the relationship between father's education and plan, a positive correlation indicated that the higher the level of father's education, the more likely the student was to attend college. The variables also were combined in regression equations and a number of multiple correlation coefficients were obtained.

For samples of the size used in this analysis, correlation coefficients can be considered statistically significant at the .05 probability level when they are above .10 and significant at the .01 level above .15.

FATHER'S OCCUPATION

Students checked the category in which the father's occupation fell, and these categories were ranked from number 1, professional, through number 7, factory worker or laborer. Students who indicated their fathers were in occupations which could not be classified easily in the seven categories on the questionnaire were not included in the analysis. Because the professionals were given the rank of 1 and the laborers the rank of 7, the resulting correlations with college attendance were negative. Correlations between father's occupation and college attendance are shown for each of the residence groups in Table 27. Since most stu-

Table 27. Coefficients of Correlation between Father's Occupational Level and College Plans

Area	Boys				Girls			
	1950		1961		1950		1961	
	Correlation	N	Correlation	N	Correlation	N	Correlation	N
Metropolitan	−.49	290	−.30*	397	−.43	345	−.33	425
Nonfarm	−.32	279	−.34	399	−.39	300	−.36	440
Farm	−.09	204	−.07	213	−.01	322	−.11	308

* Correlations for 1950 and 1961 differ significantly at .01 level.

dents living on farms had fathers who were farmers, significant correlations were not found for this variable among the farm students. Correlations for the other two area groups tended to be in the vicinity of .35, and changed significantly over the eleven-year period only among the metropolitan boys. Here the relationship of college attendance to father's occupation significantly decreased. The correlations also decreased for the metropolitan girls, but not enough to be statistically significant. Correlations among the nonfarm groups remained similar for the survey years.

FAMILY INCOME

Students in both survey years were asked to check a phrase on the questionnaire which best described their family income. The six categories ranged from "frequently have difficulty making ends meet" through "comfortable but not well-to-do" to "wealthy." The relationship of reported adequacy of income with plans to attend college is shown for each of the residence groups in Table 28. Again, no relationship

Table 28. Coefficients of Correlation between Reported Adequacy of Family Income and College Plans

| | Boys | | | | Girls | | | |
| | 1950 | | 1961 | | 1950 | | 1961 | |
Area	Corre-lation	N	Corre-lation	N	Corre-lation	N	Corre-lation	N
Metropolitan	.27	290	.24	397	.34	345	—.02*	425
Nonfarm	.20	279	.24	399	.25	300	.24	440
Farm	.09	204	.11	213	.05	322	.07	308

*Correlations for 1950 and 1961 differ significantly at .001 level.

was found among the farm groups, but among the other groups it tended to be in the vicinity of .25. This relationship did not change significantly between the two survey years except among the metropolitan girls, and the authors offer no explanation for the large drop which occurred in the relationship for this group. The low relationship found for the 1961 metropolitan girls was checked for another sample of these girls and the low correlation was found again in the second sample.

EDUCATION OF PARENTS

The students checked the highest educational level attained by each of their parents on a nine-point scale, ranging from "did not attend school" through "some high school" up to "holds more than one college degree." The correlations for each of the groups between father's educational level and whether the student planned to attend college are shown in Table 29. The correlations were generally in the vicinity of .40, except among farm students where the relationship was smaller. The relationship of father's education to college attendance dropped substantially among the metropolitan boys. Similar correlations are shown

Table 29. Coefficients of Correlation between Father's Educational Level and College Plans

	Boys				Girls			
	1950		1961		1950		1961	
Area	Corre-lation	N	Corre-lation	N	Corre-lation	N	Corre-lation	N
Metropolitan	.43	290	.15*	397	.44	345	.46	425
Nonfarm	.35	279	.50†	399	.32	300	.43	440
Farm	.12	204	.17	213	.22	322	.23	308

* Correlations for 1950 and 1961 differ significantly at .001 level.
† Correlations for 1950 and 1961 differ significantly at .05 level.

for the educational level attained by the mother in Table 30. These relationships are similar to those found for father's education, and once more are substantially lower among farm students. Again the relationship is similar for both survey years, except that the correlation for the 1961 metropolitan boys is significantly lower than that for the corresponding group in 1950. A tendency is shown in the 1961 correlations for the educational level of each parent to be more highly related to college attendance for girls than for boys. Within each group the relationship of the educational level of each parent to college attendance is quite similar. Previous studies have shown the mother's educational level to be a more important factor than that of the father in determin-

Table 30. Coefficients of Correlation between Mother's Educational Level and College Plans

	Boys				Girls			
	1950		1961		1950		1961	
Area	Corre-lation	N	Corre-lation	N	Corre-lation	N	Corre-lation	N
Metropolitan	.35	290	.17*	397	.39	345	.30	425
Nonfarm	.40	279	.32	399	.45	300	.50	440
Farm	.05	204	.20	213	.26	322	.34	308

* Correlations for 1950 and 1961 differ significantly at .05 level.

109

ing whether the student goes to college. These figures do not support that finding, but suggest that the educational level of both parents is equally important.

NUMBER OF BOOKS IN THE HOME

Correlations between the number of books the students reported in their homes and college attendance are shown for the 1961 samples in Table 31. Similar correlations for the 1950 study were not readily available. The number of books in the home showed a higher relationship to college attendance than did reported adequacy of income. The relationship was higher for both sexes and significantly so among the girls.

Table 31. Coefficients of Correlation between Reported Number of Books in the Home and College Plans of Seniors in 1961

Area	Boys, 1961		Girls, 1961	
	Corre-lation	N	Corre-lation	N
Metropolitan	.25	397	.32	425
Nonfarm	.24	399	.35	440
Farm	.17	213	.27	308

A COMBINATION OF SOCIOECONOMIC VARIABLES

The socioeconomic variables — parental occupation and educational levels and reported adequacy of income — were combined in single regression equations. The multiple correlation coefficients for these equations are shown for each sex and residence group in Table 32. Among the metropolitan and nonfarm students, the multiple correla-

Table 32. Multiple Correlation Coefficients between Four Socioeconomic Variables and College Plans

	Boys				Girls			
	1950		1961		1950		1961	
Area	Corre-lation	N	Corre-lation	N	Corre-lation	N	Corre-lation	N
Metropolitan	.54	290	.39*	397	.56	345	.52	425
Nonfarm	.45	279	.55	399	.51	300	.56	440
Farm	.15	204	.26	213	.31	322	.40	308

* Correlations for 1950 and 1961 differ significantly at .01 level.

110

tions are in the vicinity of .50. They are somewhat lower among the farm students, particularly among the boys. The relationship of these variables to college attendance did not change significantly over the intervening eleven years except among the metropolitan boys, where the relationship in 1961 was significantly lower.

The state university and other colleges are more easily accessible to metropolitan students, and among the large number of metropolitan boys now attending college socioeconomic variables have become less important as determinants of college attendance.

RELATIONSHIP OF ABILITY MEASURES

The relationship of scores on scholastic aptitude tests with college attendance also was observed for groups of both survey years. In 1950 the ACE taken in the senior year, and in 1961 the MSAT taken in the junior year, were used. The correlation coefficients between these test scores and whether the student planned to attend college or get a job are shown for each of the six groups in Table 33. The relationship of test scores to college attendance increased significantly among the girls and among the farm boys between 1950 and 1961. Ability, then, appeared to be a more important factor in college attendance in 1961 for these groups than in 1950.

Table 33. Coefficients of Correlation between Scholastic Aptitude Test
Scores and College Plans

	Boys				Girls			
	1950 (ACE)		1961 (MSAT)		1950 (ACE)		1961 (MSAT)	
Area	Corre-lation	N	Corre-lation	N	Corre-lation	N	Corre-lation	N
Metropolitan	.44	290	.32	397	.30	345	.43*	425
Nonfarm	.38	279	.39	399	.45	300	.59*	440
Farm	.29	204	.52†	213	.30	322	.47*	308

* Correlations for 1950 and 1961 differ significantly at .05 level.
† Correlations for 1950 and 1961 differ significantly at .01 level.

HIGH SCHOOL RANK

The relationship of school achievement — as measured by high school percentile rank — with college attendance is shown in Table 34. A significant increase in the relationship between high school rank and

111

college attendance was found for the farm students of both sexes. The correlations between high school rank and college attendance were similar to those between scholastic aptitude test score and college attendance. Furthermore, the changes which occurred between 1950 and 1961 were also similar for farm students. The relationship between high school rank and scholastic aptitude test scores was in the order of .60.

Table 34. Coefficients of Correlation between High School Percentile Rank and College Plans

	Boys				Girls			
	1950		1961		1950		1961	
Area	Corre-lation	N	Corre-lation	N	Corre-lation	N	Corre-lation	N
Metropolitan	.33	290	.30	397	.30	345	.39	425
Nonfarm	.40	279	.38	399	.47	300	.57	440
Farm	.44	204	.62*	213	.33	322	.53†	308

* Correlations for 1950 and 1961 differ significantly at .05 level.
† Correlations for 1950 and 1961 differ significantly at .01 level.

When high school percentile rank and scholastic aptitude test scores were combined in a regression equation to yield multiple correlation coefficients with college attendance, the results were as shown in Table 35. These regression coefficients are only slightly higher than those obtained from either of the variables alone.

Table 35. Multiple Correlation Coefficients between High School Percentile Rank — Scholastic Aptitude Test Score and College Plans

	Boys				Girls			
	1950		1961		1950		1961	
Area	Corre-lation	N	Corre-lation	N	Corre-lation	N	Corre-lation	N
Metropolitan	.46	290	.35	397	.34	345	.45	425
Nonfarm	.43	279	.42	399	.50	300	.62	440
Farm	.44	204	.63	213	.35	322	.55	308

Ability and achievement during the eleven years became more important in determining whether or not girls from all areas and boys from the farm attended college. The importance of socioeconomic factors remained constant for certain groups and for others significantly decreased during this period. These changes are undoubtedly due to the fact that more of the able students now have the opportunity to attend college. That ability and achievement factors are becoming increasingly more important than socioeconomic background as a determinant of college attendance is an encouraging trend in a democratic society.

Table 36. Multiple Correlation Coefficients between Six Achievement-Aptitude-Socioeconomic Variables and College Plans

	Boys				Girls			
	1950		1961		1950		1961	
Area	Corre-lation	N	Corre-lation	N	Corre-lation	N	Corre-lation	N
Metropolitan	.63	290	.46*	397	.60	345	.56	425
Nonfarm	.52	279	.63†	399	.61	300	.71†	440
Farm	.46	204	.64*	213	.44	322	.59*	308

* Correlations for 1950 and 1961 differ significantly at .01 level.
† Correlations for 1950 and 1961 differ significantly at .05 level.

Table 37. Correlation Coefficients between Scholastic Aptitude Test Scores and Socioeconomic Variables *

	Boys		Girls	
Area	1950	1961	1950	1961
Father's Occupational Level				
Metropolitan	−.27	−.28	−.14	−.30
Nonfarm	−.21	−.37	−.28	−.26
Farm	−.13	−.13	.04	−.11
Father's Educational Level				
Metropolitan	.31	.17	.23	.35
Nonfarm	.29	.13	.33	.29
Farm	.16	.14	.16	.26
Mother's Educational Level				
Metropolitan	.26	.21	.20	.24
Nonfarm	.32	.20	.35	.30
Farm	.14	.17	.14	.34
Income				
Metropolitan	.23	.11	.06	.00
Nonfarm	.16	.16	.12	.18
Farm	−.07	.01	.00	.00
Number of Books				
Metropolitan		.25		.42
Nonfarm		.17		.30
Farm		.17		.29

* See Tables 1–11 for sample sizes involved in these correlations.

When all seven variables — high school percentile rank, scholastic aptitude test scores, and the five socioeconomic variables — are combined in one regression equation, the coefficients which result for each of the six groups are as shown in Table 36. With the exception of the metropolitan boys, where the ability to predict college attendance from these factors has shown a significant decrease, college attendance can be predicted for the other 1961 groups at the .60 level. The significantly higher coefficients shown for the 1961 groups demonstrate the increased variance accounted for by the aptitude and achievement factors.

The meaning of these multiple correlations is clarified when one recalls that a correlation coefficient of .60 essentially accounts for 36 per cent of the variance, which explains the variability of the condition being predicted. Thus, if one can conceive of post-high-school plans as resulting from a multitude of conditions and situations, approximately

Table 38. Correlation Coefficients between High School Percentile Rank
and Socioeconomic Variables*

Variable and Area	Boys		Girls	
	1950	1961	1950	1961
Minnesota Scholastic Aptitude Test				
Metropolitan	.50	.54	.57	.68
Nonfarm	.66	.67	.68	.73
Farm	.66	.69	.68	.69
Father's Occupational Level				
Metropolitan	−.04	−.06	−.13	−.19
Nonfarm	−.34	−.25	−.28	−.30
Farm	−.13	−.07	.03	−.11
Father's Educational Level				
Metropolitan	.10	.06	.11	.31
Nonfarm	.33	.10	.27	.30
Farm	.13	.17	.08	.23
Mother's Educational Level				
Metropolitan	.14	.15	.17	.12
Nonfarm	.35	.18	.30	.32
Farm	.07	.17	.00	.22
Income				
Metropolitan	.06	.10	.15	−.09
Nonfarm	.12	.13	.08	.23
Farm	−.11	.02	.09	.03
Number of Books				
Metropolitan		.18		.31
Nonfarm		.04		.29
Farm		.13		.24

* See Tables 1–11 for sample sizes involved in these correlations.

one third of the conditions and situations are measured by these indices of ability, socioeconomic status, and high school percentile rank. This means that approximately two thirds of the variance is accounted for by other conditions, among which the most evident are sex and area. Other variables related to plans, as demonstrated in this report, are the attitudes, values, and personalities of students.

Even if socioeconomic factors had no effect on whether a student planned to attend college, these variables would still show a significant correlation with plans because of the relationships between ability and such socioeconomic factors as parental education and occupational levels. The relationships of each of the socioeconomic variables to scholastic aptitude test scores and high school rank are shown for each of the groups in Tables 37 and 38.

Father's occupational level, father's educational level, and mother's educational level all correlated with scholastic aptitude test scores at about the same level — between .20 and .30 — among the metropolitan and nonfarm groups of both sexes. Smaller relationships — between .10 and .20 — were found among the farm groups. Adequacy of family income was only slightly related (.10) to test scores, and showed no relationship among farm students. Number of books in the home showed a relationship with test scores at the .20 level for the boys and at the .30 level for the girls.

The relationship between parental occupational and educational level and high school ranks was similar to that found for test scores among the nonfarm (.20) and farm (.10) students. Correlations among the metropolitan students were in the vicinity of .10 while for test scores they were at the .20 level. Among the metropolitan students, then, these socioeconomic variables appeared to be related more to ability than to school achievement, while for the other two groups these relationships were equal. For high school ranks, as for test scores, number of books in the home showed a higher correlation for the girls than for the boys.

10

Students Bound for College

IN 1961, of the 44,756 students who expressed some post-high-school plan, 18,233, or 41 per cent, planned to attend college. These plans were related significantly to the sex of the student: 45 per cent of the boys planned on college as compared with 37 per cent of the girls. In each of the three areas more boys than girls planned to attend college as shown in the accompanying tabulation. About 10 per cent more

Area	Boys	Girls
Metropolitan	54%	45%
Nonfarm	48	38
Farm	28	25

boys than girls from the metropolitan and nonfarm areas planned to attend college while the proportions of each sex living on farms and planning on college were about equal. The proportion of college-bound metropolitan students, 50 per cent, was about twice as large as that for farm students, 26 per cent. The proportion for the nonfarm students — 43 per cent — fell in between, tending more toward the metropolitan group.

In 1950 a slight relationship was found between age and college attendance: a larger proportion of younger than of older students planned to attend college. In 1961, when the students completed the questionnaire in January of their senior year, 83 per cent of the college-bound boys, and 73 per cent of the employment-bound, were seventeen years old. Only 12 per cent of the college-planning boys were eighteen years old as compared with 22 per cent of the job-seeking boys. Similar but smaller differences were found for the girls.

Father's occupation was closely related to college plans. Among the

116

nonfarm boys planning on college, 13 per cent had fathers in the professions while only 2 per cent of those seeking jobs did.

Parents' education was also closely related to post-high-school plans. Among the nonfarm boys, of those planning on college 20 per cent had fathers who were college graduates as compared with only 2 per cent of those who planned on jobs; 23 per cent who planned on college, and 54 per cent who planned to get jobs, had fathers with no more than an eighth-grade education. Similar differences were found among students of both sexes and from all residence areas.

Among the metropolitan students of both sexes, about 25 per cent had parents who had graduated from high school but had no further formal education. If their parents had any education beyond high school the children tended to go to college; if their parents were not high school graduates, fewer of them planned to enter college. Educational levels of fathers were highest in the metropolitan areas and lowest in farm areas. Among the college-bound students 13 per cent had fathers with no more than an eighth-grade education, as compared with 23 per cent in the nonfarm areas and 54 per cent in the farm areas. Eight per cent of the college-bound farm boys, and 37 per cent of the college-bound metropolitan students, had fathers who had some college training. The educational level of fathers in the 1961 survey was higher than that of fathers in 1950. Of the metropolitan college-bound boys, 22 per cent in 1950, and only 13 per cent in 1961, had fathers with no more than an eighth-grade education. In 1950, 17 per cent of the metropolitan college-bound boys had fathers who were high school graduates but had taken no further training as compared with 26 per cent of this group in 1961.

The relationship between college plans and mother's educational level was similar to that for father's educational level. Among college-bound students of both sexes from both metropolitan and nonfarm areas, 16 per cent had mothers who were college graduates as opposed to only 3 per cent of the students seeking employment. Among college-bound students the proportion with mothers who had not graduated from high school was much smaller than the proportion with fathers who had not graduated from high school. As was true for the educational level of fathers, the level of maternal education in 1961 was higher than in 1950, but the relationship with post-high-school plans was similar. Again educational levels were highest among urban mothers, next highest among nonfarm mothers, and lowest among farm mothers.

FAMILY INCOME

College attendance is strongly related to source of family income. Among metropolitan boys, 17 per cent of the college-bound, and only 6 per cent of the job seekers, came from families whose principal source of income was professional fees or business profits. Of the students from families whose income was from salaries, the percentage planning on college was twice as great as the percentage seeking employment, although this difference was reversed where family income was based on hourly or daily wages. The relationships were similar for both sexes.

These differences, of course, do not hold true for farm students, where farm profit represents the principal source of income for the families of over two thirds of the students. Even among these students, however, differences in this direction do occur. For 74 per cent of college-bound students from the farm the principal source of family income was farm profits, while a lower proportion, 64 per cent, of those planning to seek jobs came from such families. Among students who live on farms, of those planning on employment 20 per cent had fathers working for hourly wages, almost twice the 11 per cent who planned to attend college.

Responses on adequacy of family income showed a significant relationship to college attendance, but as was true in 1950 the relationship was much smaller than might be expected. Among the nonfarm boys, 3 per cent of those going to college said their families frequently had difficulties making ends meet, as compared with 9 per cent of those seeking jobs. On the other hand, 61 per cent of the college-bound students felt their families were comfortably well off financially, as compared with 47 per cent of those seeking jobs. These differences were similar among both boys and girls from both the metropolitan and nonfarm areas. In 1950 the percentage of college-bound students from the farm who checked each of the response categories was similar to that of students from other areas. The farm students of 1961 felt their family income was significantly less adequate than those of 1950, and about 10 per cent fewer college-bound farm students than those from other areas felt their families had a comfortable income.

118

SIZE OF HOME

There was a slight tendency for college-bound students to come from homes with ten or more rooms rather than from homes with four or five rooms. All differences in size of home were small and there were none among students from the farm. The differences found on this variable in 1950 were equally small. More college-bound students than those with other plans reported having an unshared bedroom, and this is true for both sexes from all residence areas. Among the metropolitan boys 59 per cent of those planning on college had bedrooms of their own as compared with 48 per cent of those planning to seek employment. Number of people in the home was not related to post-high-school plans.

CULTURAL STATUS OF HOME

Students planning to attend college reported many more books in their homes than those with other plans. Among nonfarm boys planning on college, 38 per cent reported more than 100 books, as compared with only 16 per cent of the nonfarm boys planning on employment. Twelve per cent of the nonfarm boys seeking jobs reported less than 10 books, as compared with 2 per cent of those planning on college. Regions, but not sexes, showed differences in number of books reported by college-bound students. Forty-six per cent of the metropolitan, 38 per cent of the nonfarm, and 26 per cent of the farm students planning on college reported more than 100 books in the home. At the same time, 9 per cent of the metropolitan, 12 per cent of the nonfarm, and 19 per cent of the farm college-bound students reported fewer than 25 books. Proportions of college-bound students reporting various numbers of books in 1961 were almost exactly the same as the proportions in 1950. Differences between the various regions also remained the same.

For many of the magazines surveyed, the proportions of college-bound students reporting them in their homes also remained similar. Although metropolitan and nonfarm groups reported differences in number of books, these differences were much smaller for most of the magazines surveyed. The farm groups remained different from the others in numbers and types of magazines. Several farm magazines were taken by a large majority of the farm families, and of the three farm magazines at least one was found in almost 75 per cent of the farm

119

homes — a larger coverage than that for the *Reader's Digest* and *Life* in any of the areas. Sixty-five per cent of the college-bound metropolitan and nonfarm students reported the *Reader's Digest*, as compared with 55 per cent of college-bound students from the farm. The *Saturday Evening Post* was checked by 35 per cent of the metropolitan, 41 per cent of the nonfarm, and 29 per cent of the farm students. Large differences continued to be found in the magazines checked by students with various post-high-school plans. Twenty per cent fewer students in each of the regions who planned to get jobs checked the *Reader's Digest*, as compared with those bound for college. *Time* was checked by 29 per cent of the metropolitan, 21 per cent of the nonfarm, and 10 per cent of the farm college-bound students, while for those seeking jobs the percentages were 11, 8, and 5 respectively. Differences were not found for magazines such as *True, Argosy, Sports Afield, Popular Mechanics,* and *Popular Science.*

Students planning to attend college more often reported their parents were members of various typical organizations than students with other plans. The only exceptions to this pattern were labor unions and the Farmers Union, organizations with which parents of college-bound students were less likely to be associated. The parents of metropolitan boys were more likely to be members of the PTA (64 per cent) than parents of nonfarm (54 per cent) or farm (56 per cent) boys. Parents of metropolitan girls were even more likely to be members of this organization, with 74 per cent being members of the PTA. No sex differences were found for the other two regions. Membership in veterans' organizations was more typical of nonfarm parents than of metropolitan or farm parents. The largest number of students reporting their parents were members of a labor union came from the metropolitan area, nonfarm students were next, and the smallest number was found among the farm students. Mothers' membership in the ladies' aid reversed this relationship. Over half the farm students had mothers in this organization, as compared with a third from nonfarm areas and less than 10 per cent from the metropolitan area. Church organizations showed similar relationships, but the differences were smaller.

Large differences were found in membership in organizations between parents of college-bound students and parents of other groups. Sixty-four per cent of the college-bound metropolitan boys, and 34 per cent of those planning to seek employment, reported their parents were members of the PTA. Twenty-nine per cent of the nonfarm girls planning on college, and 17 per cent of those seeking jobs, reported their parents were members of a neighborhood club. Similar results were found for nonfarm boys. Over 50 per cent of the farm students planning on college said their parents were members of the ladies' aid, as compared with 40 per cent of those seeking jobs, and for church organizations these proportions were 70 per cent for the college-bound farm students and 55 per cent for the job seekers.

These relationships between membership in organizations and college attendance were similar to those found in the 1950 survey, with a few noteworthy differences. Membership in PTA groups did not change significantly among the parents of metropolitan college-bound students, but it increased significantly in the nonfarm and farm areas. The PTA groups apparently increased in membership in the outlying areas during the eleven-year period. Membership in veterans' organizations decreased, and membership in the ladies' aid decreased considerably in the metropolitan and nonfarm areas, but remained strong among the parents of college-bound farm students. In 1950 the proportion of college-bound students whose fathers belonged to a labor union included about 25 per cent of the metropolitan students and smaller proportions of students from other areas. This proportion in 1961 remained about the same for the metropolitan area, but increased for other areas, particularly among students living on farms.

FINANCIAL AID FROM FAMILY

Fifteen per cent of the college-bound boys and 10 per cent of the girls said they would receive no financial help from their families in meeting their college expenses. These proportions, similar among students from all residence areas, represented a slight increase in the proportion receiving no family help in 1961 over 1950. Among the boys the increase was small, from 12 per cent in 1950 to 15 per cent in 1961, but it rose substantially among the girls, from 5 per cent in 1950 to 10 per cent in 1961.

Some students expected their parents to pay all their college expenses; 20 per cent of the metropolitan and nonfarm girls and 13 per cent of the farm girls expected complete financial aid. This figure was only

121

about 8 per cent for the boys from all areas. The proportion expecting their parents to pay all expenses decreased substantially over the period, particularly among girls. In 1950 these percentages were 34 per cent for the metropolitan and nonfarm girls and 28 per cent for the farm girls, and among the boys the proportion was 12 per cent from all areas. About a third of the girls and a quarter of the boys expected their parents to pay most of their expenses and about half of the boys and a third of the girls expected their families to pay some of their college expenses. As a whole, for college-bound students from all areas and of both sexes, the trend over the eleven years was toward expecting less financial help from family sources.

FAMILY'S ATTITUDE TOWARD COLLEGE

Eighty-two per cent of the college-bound students reported their parents "wanted" them to attend college. This proportion was the same for both sexes and for all residence areas. This was also substantially the same proportion of students indicating this family attitude in 1950. Differences did occur, however, in proportions reporting other types of family attitudes, either insistence that the student attend college or indifference to his going. Fifteen per cent of the 1961 college-bound metropolitan and nonfarm boys, and only 9 per cent of those from the farm, reported their parents insisted on college. This figure of 9 per cent from the farm represents a substantial increase over the 4 per cent reported in 1950. The proportions among the metropolitan and nonfarm groups did not change over this period. Somewhat fewer girls reported their parents insisted that they attend college — 10 per cent of the metropolitan and nonfarm girls and 4 per cent of the farm girls. These proportions were similar to those reported in 1950.

Only among the boys from farms was there a substantial number — 10 per cent — stating parental indifference to their going to college, and among the nonfarm boys only 2 per cent, considerably smaller than the figures reported in 1950, when 19 per cent from the farm and 5 per cent of the others reported parental indifference. More girls than boys felt their parents were indifferent to their attending college — 12 per cent of the college-bound farm girls and 7 per cent of the others. These proportions among the girls did not change over the decade. Almost none of the students planning on college said their parents did not want

122

them to attend; only among farm students of both sexes did 1 per cent indicate this family attitude.

EDUCATIONAL BACKGROUND AND PLANS

Differences in types of high school curriculums taken by college-bound students occurred both between sexes and between regions. The meaning of these differences is confused by the fact that many smaller high schools do not have clearly differentiated curriculums. College-bound boys were more likely to take a college-preparatory curriculum than college-bound girls. Metropolitan students were more likely to take a college-preparatory program than nonfarm students, and nonfarm students were more likely to than farm students, as shown in the accompanying tabulation.

Area	Boys	Girls
Metropolitan	80%	76%
Nonfarm	76	72
Farm	70	63

The proportions of college-bound students taking college-preparatory programs increased only slightly in the metropolitan areas but increased greatly for the nonfarm and farm regions in the eleven years after 1950. Forty-five per cent of the college-bound boys and 39 per cent of the college-bound girls from the farm took college-preparatory curriculums in 1950, as compared with 70 per cent and 63 per cent, respectively, in 1961. Most college-bound students not taking a preparatory course indicated they took a general program. Nine per cent of the college-bound girls and 2 per cent of the boys took commercial curriculums in high school. Six per cent of the college-bound boys from the farm took agricultural curriculums, a considerable decrease from the 11 per cent taking this curriculum in 1950. Increased variety of high school curriculums, clearer differentiation between curriculums, as well as more and better guidance in the nonmetropolitan schools probably led to this increase in the proportions of nonmetropolitan college-bound students taking preparatory courses.

Students were asked to check the reasons why they adopted the curriculum they took in high school. The proportion of college-bound students giving "counselor's advice" increased from approximately 8 per cent in 1950 to 20 per cent in 1961. Those who said they had no choice because their curriculum was the only one offered in their high school were 18 per cent from the farm group and 9 per cent from the nonfarm group in 1950, while in 1961 these proportions had dropped to 6 per cent for the farm group and 3 per cent for the nonfarm group. The reason most often given was that the curriculum fitted their vocational plans the best, checked by 60 per cent of the boys and 68 per cent of the girls. About a third said these courses were the most interesting to them, and about a fourth gave parental advice as an important reason.

Approximately 75 per cent of the boys and 80 per cent of the girls gave "preparation for a vocation" as one of the most important reasons for planning to attend college. For both sexes, proportions checking this item were slightly higher among the nonfarm and the farm groups. About a third checked "getting a liberal education" as a reason for going to college; this reason was more likely to be checked by metropolitan students than by those from other regions. About a third of the boys and a fifth of the girls gave "will enable me to make more money" as one of their reasons. Twenty per cent of the girls gave the fact that they liked school as a reason, while this was checked by only 10 per cent of the boys.

Large differences were found between both sexes and regions on the item asking the college-bound students if they were considering going on with any graduate or professional training after completing their undergraduate college work. This item was answered in the affirmative by 49 per cent of the metropolitan boys, 43 per cent of the nonfarm boys, and 34 per cent of the farm boys. Among the girls these proportions were 29, 24, and 20 per cent respectively. Among the boys, science was the area of graduate training most often given, mentioned by 8 per cent. Proportions checking further work in science were similar in all residence areas. Professional training in medicine or law was mentioned by 5 per cent of the metropolitan boys, 4 per cent of the nonfarm boys, and 2 per cent of the farm boys. Education was the most frequently mentioned graduate area for the girls — 4 per cent as compared with 2 per cent of the boys.

INFLUENCE OF MARRIAGE ON PLANS

Fewer college-bound students than others said that marriage influenced their plans for the coming year. Three per cent of the boys and

124

5 per cent of the girls, however, said that the prospect of marriage did influence their plans. This compares with 10 per cent for the boys and 25 per cent for the girls who planned to seek jobs on graduation. Less than 1 per cent of the college-bound students were already married or planned to be married on graduation from high school. One per cent of the girls and less than 1 per cent of the boys said they planned to be married a year after graduation. Sixty-four per cent of the boys and 57 per cent of the girls had no idea when they might get married. The college-bound group had the smallest proportions definitely planning on marriage of any of the plan groups in the survey. There were considerable differences between boys and girls on marriage plans as a variable, but no difference between residence areas.

11

Students Seeking Jobs

ABOUT one fourth of the 1961 graduating high school seniors indicated they planned to enter the labor market upon graduation from high school. Over twice as many girls as boys planned to get jobs, 32 per cent as opposed to 15 per cent. These proportions also varied considerably by residence area. For the boys, these proportions planned to seek jobs: metropolitan, 12 per cent; nonfarm, 15 per cent; and farm, 21 per cent. For the girls, these figures were 30, 29, and 40 per cent respectively. As was discussed in a previous chapter, the proportions planning to seek employment, especially among the boys, were considerably smaller than in 1950.

Another 3 per cent of all graduates, those who planned to work for their parents upon graduation, are not included in this discussion. This group consisted primarily of the 15 per cent of the farm boys and 8 per cent of the farm girls planning to work at home.

APTITUDE AND ACHIEVEMENT

Mean aptitude test scores were lower for students planning on jobs than for students with other plans. For example, among the nonfarm boys, those planning to get a job had a mean MSAT score of 23, a percentile rank of 39 for high school students and of 14 for college entrants.

The differences found between plan groups on aptitude test scores resembled those found between plan groups on high school rank. The mean high school rank for those seeking employment was 30 for boys and 47 for girls. Students seeking employment tended to have lower mean high school percentile ranks than groups planning on other activities.

126

AGE

The median age for students planning on employment was 17.6 years. A slightly higher proportion of job-seeking students were 18 years or older, but generally speaking, there were no meaningful differences between the ages of students planning to seek employment and those with other plans.

FATHER'S OCCUPATION

Among the job-seeking students of both sexes from the metropolitan areas, about one third had fathers in the skilled trades, and about one fourth had fathers who were laborers or factory workers. In the non-farm areas the proportions were more equal, running between 25 and 30 per cent in each of the two occupational categories. Naturally, most of those living on farms and planning to work came from homes where the father was a farmer. These proportions did not change significantly over the eleven years. Only 2 per cent of the job-seeking students not living on farms had fathers in professional occupations. In 1950 this proportion was 4 per cent, so that the proportion of job-seeking students with fathers in the professions dropped about one half after 1950, this drop being consistent among students of both sexes and from each of the residence areas. There was a significant tendency for students from farms to be more likely to seek employment if their fathers were not engaged in farming and were in skilled trades or laboring occupations, fields in which nonfarming parents who live on farms are most often employed. Students from these homes were more likely to seek employment than to continue their education. Students seeking employment were more likely than the others to come from homes where the father held a lower level job such as skilled tradesman or laborer. Although substantial changes were found in parental occupation over the eleven years among students with other plans, the proportion of the job seekers reporting various types of parental occupations remained substantially the same. The exception here was the proportion of farm students reporting the father as engaged in farming, which dropped considerably for students in all the plan groups.

EDUCATION OF PARENTS

The median educational level of the fathers of job-seeking students was "some high school" for those from the metropolitan area, and an

127

eighth-grade education for the nonfarm and farm groups. The job planners had the most fathers with no more than an eighth-grade education, and the proportion with an eighth-grade education or less was much higher than for students planning to attend college. Among nonfarm males, 54 per cent of the job seekers had fathers with no more than an eighth-grade education, as compared with only 23 per cent of those planning on college. Among job seekers of both sexes, about 10 per cent of the metropolitan, 5 per cent of the nonfarm, and 2 per cent of the farm students had parents with some college education. Among the college-going students these percentages were 37 per cent, 30 per cent, and 8 per cent respectively. There were no real differences between the sexes among students seeking employment. Parents from the metropolitan areas were better educated than nonfarm parents, who in turn had considerably more education than those from farms. Educational levels of parents of job seekers increased considerably over the intervening eleven years, as did the educational levels of all parents. In the metropolitan areas the principal increase was in fathers with a high school education, with a corresponding decline in fathers with an eighth-grade education; in the farm areas the largest increase was in fathers who had completed the eighth grade, with a decline in fathers with less than an eighth-grade education. The proportion of job-seeking students with college-educated parents increased only slightly in the decade after 1950.

The modal level of the job seekers' mothers was high school graduation for the metropolitan group, some high school for the nonfarm group, and completion of the eighth grade for the farm group; this level was also lower than that for all other plan groups, and considerably lower than that for mothers of students planning on college. Of the nonfarm boys, 7 per cent of the job seekers had mothers who had some college training, as compared with 32 per cent of those planning on college.

FAMILY INCOME

Of the metropolitan job-planning students of both sexes, 66 per cent gave the principal source of family income as hourly or daily wages. For the nonfarm group this figure was 54 per cent. In both the metropolitan and nonfarm areas, roughly twice the proportion of students whose family income is derived either from professional fees and profits or salary go to college as seek jobs, while about twice the proportion of those whose family income is from wages seek jobs as opposed to attending college.

With the exception of students from the farm, the proportions reporting specific types of family income among the job seekers did not change between 1950 and 1961. As would be expected, the proportion from farms where the chief source of income is farm profits decreased during this period. Among families living on the farm, if the source of income is not farm profits it is likely to be wages, and the students from these families were more likely to seek employment than plan for further education.

More job-seeking students than others reported family income to be inadequate. Among both the metropolitan and nonfarm job seekers of both sexes, 15 to 18 per cent reported either that their family frequently had difficulty making ends meet, or that they sometimes lacked necessities. This percentage is about three times the 5 to 6 per cent of the college-bound students reporting this description of family income. As was true for most other plan groups, about the same proportion reported a comfortable income as in 1950, but fewer checked the answer "Have all the necessities but not many luxuries," and this drop was made up by more frequent checking of the two "less than adequate" income descriptions.

In general, then, in regard to occupational, educational, and economic status, job-seeking students tended to be slightly lower on each of these indices than students with most other types of plans, and considerably below the status of the college-bound seniors.

SIZE OF HOME

Boys seeking employment came from four-to-five-room homes slightly more often than most other students. Of the metropolitan boys, 19 per cent came from five-room homes as compared with 12 per cent of those planning on college and 16 per cent of those going to trade school. On the other hand, only 5 per cent of these metropolitan boys came from homes with more than eleven rooms, as compared with 11 per cent of those planning on college. Similar differences were found in each of the other residence areas. Among the girls the same types of differences

129

were found between girls seeking jobs and those planning on college, but smaller differences in size of home were found between girls planning on post-high-school training other than college and those seeking jobs. About half the job seekers of both sexes had an unshared bedroom. This proportion was similar to that for students with other plans except those planning on college, of whom 60 per cent had a bedroom to themselves. These figures were similar to those of 1950. No relationship was found between the number of people in the home and whether the student sought employment or made other plans.

CULTURAL STATUS OF HOME

Among those of both sexes planning on jobs, 7 per cent of the metropolitan, 12 per cent of the nonfarm, and 14 per cent of the farm students reported fewer than 10 books in their homes. This is a larger proportion than for any other type of plan, and differs greatly from the group planning on college, where, for example, among the nonfarm students only 2 per cent of college planners reported fewer than 10 books, as compared with 14 per cent of those seeking employment. Conversely, the proportion of job seekers reporting more than 100 books is smaller than that of other students, and much smaller than the proportion of those planning on college. For metropolitan students, a quarter of the job seekers reported more than 100 books in contrast to almost half the college planners.

On number of magazines in the home, smaller proportions of job seekers than of students with other plans checked the various magazines listed on the questionnaire. For almost any magazine, the highest proportion reporting it was among the college planners, the smallest among those seeking jobs. For the *Reader's Digest* a very large difference occurred between the two groups — 65 per cent of the college-going students reported it, and 48 per cent of those planning on jobs. This relationship did not exist for the farm magazines, or for magazines such as *True* and *Argosy*.

Fewer job seekers than other students reported their parents to be members of organizations, particularly students planning on college. These differences did not occur for a number of the fraternal organizations. Job seekers had the highest proportion of parents belonging to labor unions.

130

REASONS FOR PLANS

In type of high school curriculum large differences between the sexes, but few regional differences, were found among students who planned to get jobs. Almost half the boys (45 per cent) took the general curriculum, while more than half (55 per cent) the girls took a commercial program. About 27 per cent of the boys took a shop course, 10 per cent a college preparatory course, and 6 per cent a commercial program. These percentages were slightly smaller among farm boys seeking jobs, as about a fifth of them took an agricultural curriculum. A third of the girls took a general curriculum, and 7 per cent a college preparatory program.

More than half the girls who planned on getting jobs had taken courses which provided some direct occupational preparation, as compared with fewer than one third of the boys.

The proportion of students planning on jobs who took college-preparatory or general curriculums in high school decreased considerably in the period, while the proportion of job seekers who took shop courses almost doubled. Thus many more of the boys were receiving some occupational preparation in high school in 1961 than was the case in 1950. Only 20 per cent of the boys had taken vocationally relevant courses in 1950, as opposed to over a third in 1961. Better guidance in selection of high school curriculums than was available in 1950, and more vocational curriculums, may account for this.

The differences between the boys and girls in occupational training received are reflected in the reasons reported for taking the chosen curriculums. Half of the girls, and a fourth of the boys, chose their curriculum as the one best suited to their vocational plans. Approximately a third of the students of each sex indicated that it seemed the most interesting, and about 20 per cent said they did their best work in courses of these types and chose them accordingly. Eighteen per cent of the girls, and 12 per cent of the boys, checked "Parent's advice." "Counselor's advice" was the reason given by approximately 10 per cent of these students, this proportion being more than double that for 1950.

The reason most often given for planning on a job, that it enabled them to start making money quickly, was checked by one third of the metropolitan, 40 per cent of the nonfarm, and 45 per cent of the farm students of both sexes. Desire to be independent was checked by over a third of the girls and by a fourth of the boys. Preparation for a vocation was checked by 23 per cent of the boys and 18 per cent of the girls.

ATTITUDE TOWARD COLLEGE

Among girls planning on employment, about 27 per cent said they would attend college if they had more money. Although this proportion did not vary significantly in the three types of residence area, it represented a significant drop from the 35 per cent in 1950 who said they would change their plans and attend college if they had more money.

In 1950 about 44 per cent of the boys planning on jobs reported they would attend college if they could afford it, with only small regional differences on this question. In 1961 only 11 per cent of the metropolitan job seekers said they would attend college if they had more money. Among the nonfarm boys this figure was 38 per cent, and among the farm boys, 29 per cent. Large regional differences thus appeared among the boys in the present survey. With the exception of the metropolitan boys, the job-seeking students more often than the others said they would change their plans and attend college if they could afford it. The proportion of boys seeking employment after high school has decreased substantially in the metropolitan areas, so that only 12 per cent actually seek jobs after high school. Apparently college has become more accessible to this group so that most who wish to can afford to go. Most of those planning on jobs would seek employment regardless of their financial status.

The students who said they would go to college if they had more money were asked how much more they would need. About 50 per cent said they would need enough to cover all college expenses; about 43 per cent, enough to pay half; and 6 per cent, enough to pay less than half. These proportions, substantially the same for both sexes and from all regions, were also about the same as those reported in 1950.

When the students planning on employment were asked if they could afford to go to college if they wished to, 10 per cent said they could easily afford it, and 20 per cent said they could barely afford it. Thirty per cent said they could afford it but it would involve many sacrifices, and 40 per cent said they could not afford college. Similar for both sexes and for all three residence areas, these figures also were substantially the same as those for 1950.

Many of the male job seekers planned to attend college at some later date, with large regional differences among these planners. Of the metropolitan boys 33 per cent planned on eventually going to college, as compared with 27 per cent of the nonfarm and 19 per cent of the farm boys. About half of these boys planned to attend college after one year, about a fourth after two years, and the remaining fourth after three or more years.

The proportions of job-seeking girls planning on college at a later date were much smaller — 14 per cent of the metropolitan, 15 per cent of the nonfarm, and 11 per cent of the farm girls. About two thirds of these girls planned to attend college after a year, and most of the remainder after two years. Few of the girls who planned eventually to attend college intended to do so after an interval of more than two years.

Because mean ability levels of the job-seeking students were well below those of students who planned to enter college, many of these college plans were unlikely to materialize, and, undoubtedly, large numbers of these students would have found college work difficult. Nevertheless, since far fewer farm students than others made these plans, and more boys than girls, the eventual college attendance of these students would make even larger the disproportions in college attendance found between regions and sexes.

FAMILY'S ATTITUDE TOWARD COLLEGE

Two per cent of the boys and less than 1 per cent of the girls who planned to get jobs said their parents insisted that they attend college, and these proportions were similar for each region. Over half (55 per cent) of the metropolitan boys said their parents wanted them to attend college. For the nonfarm men this proportion was 48 per cent, for farm men 34 per cent. There was a very large difference between residence areas in the proportion reporting their parents as wanting them to attend college. Among the girls these differences were much smaller, 34 per cent for the metropolitan girls, 32 per cent for the nonfarm girls, and 23 per cent for the farm girls. Fewer girls than boys said their parents wanted them to attend college. At the same time, 8 per cent of the girls said their parents did not want them to attend college, as compared with 3 per cent of the boys. Many more job-seeking students than others reported parental indifference as to whether they attended col-

133

lege. The proportions of job seekers whose parents wanted them to attend college were similar to those reported in 1950.

INFLUENCE OF MARRIAGE ON PLANS

More job seekers than other students said that marriage or the early prospect of marriage had influenced their plans. Ten per cent of the boys and 25 per cent of the girls who planned on jobs said that marriage had influenced their plans, and these proportions were similar for students from each of the residence areas. Almost as many students going to trade or business school, however, said marriage influenced their plans. The big difference here occurred between those planning on college or entering nursing and those getting jobs. For metropolitan students going to college, 3 per cent of the boys and 6 per cent of the girls said marriage had influenced their plans, as compared with 11 per cent of the boys and 26 per cent of the girls who planned to seek employment.

Although a tenth of the boys and a fourth of the girls seeking jobs said that marriage had influenced their plans, many of these students had no immediate plans for marriage. One per cent of the job seekers were already married, and 1 per cent of the boys and 5 per cent of the girls planned to be married the year they graduated. Two per cent of the boys and 10 per cent of the girls planned to be married the year following graduation. Only about half the students who reported marriage as an influence planned to marry within a year and a half after graduation. More girls planning on jobs than other girls anticipated earlier marriage, and to a far greater extent than college-bound girls. The boys planning to marry either the year of graduation or in the following year were a little more likely to plan on getting jobs. For the vast majority of the boys, however, there were few differences in marriage plans among those undertaking different types of activities after graduation.

12

Plans of High-Ability Students

IN THE 1950 study special attention was given to the plans of high-ability students — the 3939 students who achieved a score of 120 or above on the American Council on Education Psychological Examination (ACE). They represented the top 18 per cent of the high school seniors for whom data were available. A comparable sample from the 1961 group included all students scoring 45 or above on the Minnesota Scholastic Aptitude Test (MSAT). In this group were 7351 students, or 17 per cent of the 1961 seniors.

The 1961 high-ability group contained more girls (54.9 per cent) than boys (45.1 per cent). This difference was due to the scholastic aptitude test used; the MSAT is a test of verbal aptitudes on which girls excel. In 1950 the ACE was used, a test containing both verbal and quantitative material, and the sex ratio was more nearly equal: 51.6 per cent were girls and 48.4 per cent boys.

The proportions of students from different regions in the high-ability samples also varied. In the total population of students surveyed, regardless of ability, 36.6 per cent were included in the metropolitan groups, while 45.4 per cent of the high-ability students came from the metropolitan area. On the other hand, while 27.0 per cent of all students lived on farms only 16.2 per cent of the high-ability students lived on farms. In 1950 the nonfarm group, not the metropolitan group, contributed a proportion of high-ability students larger than was expected — 36.5 per cent of all students surveyed in 1950 came from these non-farm areas. This change of region for high-ability students over the eleven-year period is difficult to explain. Migration to the metropolitan areas and inclusion in the metropolitan sample of suburban areas during this time might account for small differences, but it is doubtful that these factors alone would account for so large a difference.

PLANS

A comparison of the plans of high-ability students for the two survey years is shown by sex and residence area in Table 16 in Chapter 6. Eighty-one per cent of high-ability students planned to attend college in 1961, as compared with 67 per cent in 1950, an increase of 14 percentage points. Eight per cent planned to obtain jobs as compared with 18 per cent eleven years earlier. The largest increase of able students attending college occurred among the farm boys, with an increase of 21 percentage points, from 61 to 82 per cent. Although the proportion of able girls from the farm attending college increased by 13 percentage points over the eleven-year period, these girls still went to college in considerably smaller proportions in 1961 than any other group.

Ninety per cent of the able metropolitan boys planned to attend college and only 3 per cent planned to seek jobs. The increase in the proportion of high-ability students attending college was three times that for the total sample of high school seniors.

AGE

At the time of the completion of the questionnaires over 85 per cent of the high-ability students were seventeen years of age; approximately 10 per cent were eighteen, and 5 per cent were sixteen. This is a slightly larger proportion of seventeen-year-olds and a slightly smaller proportion of eighteen-year-olds than was found in the total sample of seniors. The differences between the high-ability students and the total sample were similar in direction to, but considerably smaller than, those found in 1950. The 1961 high-ability group also showed an age variability smaller than that of 1950. They were more likely to be seventeen in 1961 and less likely to be either sixteen or eighteen. Approximately 15 per cent of the girls and 10 per cent of the boys were sixteen years of age in 1950 as compared with less than 5 per cent of both sexes in 1961.

FATHER'S OCCUPATION

As with the total population surveyed, father's occupation had a relationship to the post-high-school plans of high-ability students. Among the college-bound (excluding those from farms) 20 per cent had fathers

136

in the professions; among the job seekers, approximately 4 per cent. On the other hand, a third of the job-seeking boys came from skilled tradesmen's homes, as compared with 17 per cent of the college-bound.

The high-ability boys who lived on farms were more likely to attend college if their father owned or operated the farm than they were if he was employed in some other type of occupation. Seventy-five per cent of the farm boys planning on college, and 52 per cent of those planning on jobs, said their fathers owned or operated a farm.

Similar differences were found between college-bound and job-seeking high-ability girls. Approximately 50 per cent of the girls seeking jobs came from homes where the father was a skilled tradesman or laborer, while less than one third of the college-bound girls came from workmen's homes.

The differences between college-bound and job-seeking high-ability students with regard to father's occupation remained similar to those found in 1950. In other words, although the proportion of high-ability students planning to enter college increased considerably and the proportion planning to seek jobs decreased considerably after 1950, the relationship between post-high-school plans and father's occupation remained substantially the same. Among high-ability college-bound students from the metropolitan and the nonfarm areas, approximately a fifth of the students came from professional families, for another fifth the father owned or managed a business, for about a tenth the father was engaged in sales, and for almost a third the father was a skilled tradesman or laborer.

EDUCATION OF PARENTS

The median educational level of the fathers of high-ability students from the metropolitan area was high school graduation for those who planned to seek employment and some training beyond high school for those planning on college. For fathers of students from the nonfarm area, it was some high school for the job seekers and high school graduation for the college-bound; for students from the farm it was an eighth-grade education for students with either plan. Both sexes were approximately four times as likely to attend college than seek jobs if their parents were college graduates.

Although the proportion of high-ability students attending college in-

137

creased substantially over the eleven-year period, and the proportion seeking jobs decreased considerably, the relationship of college attendance to parental educational level remained substantially the same for high-ability students in the two studies. Among nonfarm boys in 1961 whose fathers had only an eighth-grade education, 38 per cent planned on jobs and 16 per cent on attending college; in 1950 these figures were 39 and 19 per cent respectively. Since a larger proportion of high-ability students attended college and smaller proportions sought employment in 1961, we are talking about 16 per cent of a much larger proportion going on to college, and 38 per cent of a much smaller number seeking jobs, even though the ratio of the two percentages remains similar.

High-ability students tended to come from families with higher educational levels than students with similar plans in the total sample. Fathers of 50 per cent of the high-ability college-bound metropolitan boys had some college training, as compared with 27 per cent for college-bound boys in the total metropolitan sample. Mothers of high-ability students were also better educated than those of the total sample. Twenty-eight per cent of the mothers of all college-bound metropolitan boys had attended college, as compared with 38 per cent for college-bound metropolitan boys in the high-ability group. Eight per cent of all metropolitan boys seeking jobs had mothers who had been to college, as compared with 14 per cent of the high-ability metropolitan boys seeking jobs.

Among high-ability students from the farm there was a large sex difference in the educational levels of the mothers of job-seeking students: 6 per cent of the boys had college-trained mothers, as compared with 17 per cent of the girls. Of college-bound students from the farm, 33 per cent of the boys and 31 per cent of the girls had mothers who had attended college. Considerably fewer fathers than mothers of high-ability farm students had received college training. Ten per cent of the college-bound students of both sexes from the farm had fathers with some college training, and 3 per cent of the job-seeking boys and 6 per cent of the job-seeking girls had fathers with college training. Among students from the farm, then, the mother was more likely to have attended college than the father. If either parent had college training, the sons were likely to attend college, but high-ability girls were somewhat less likely to attend than boys. Proportions of high-ability students whose mothers had less than a high school education decreased substantially between

138

1950 and 1961, while the proportions with mothers who were high school graduates increased. Proportions of high-ability students planning on college or employment whose mothers had attended college both remained substantially the same in the two surveys.

FAMILY INCOME

Family income continued to be strongly related to college attendance for the high-ability group, although this relationship had decreased somewhat over that found in 1950. In 1961, for the metropolitan boys, 17 per cent of the college-bound and 12 per cent of the job seekers came from families where the principal income was from professional fees or business profits. Forty-seven per cent of the college-bound students came from homes where the income was from a fixed salary, as compared with 32 per cent of the job seekers. The proportion coming from homes where the source of income was wages was twice as great among the job-seeking students — 54 per cent — as it was for the college-bound students — 26 per cent. In 1961 a higher proportion of the high-ability college-bound students came from families of wage earners than was the case in 1950. This increase in the proportion of high-ability students from the homes of wage earners who attended college was the principal reason for the decrease in relationship of family income to college attendance. Among the high-ability farm students there was an increased tendency to attend college for students from farms where the principal income was derived from farm profits. In homes where source of income was not farm profits, and tended to be hourly or daily wages, farm students were less likely to attend college.

Reported adequacy of family income was also related to the post-high-school plans of high-ability students. Among the nonfarm boys, 9 per cent of the college-bound said they were from well-to-do families, while none of the job seekers reported this level of family income. Sixty per cent of the nonfarm college-bound students reported a "comfortable" income, as compared with 43 per cent of those seeking employment. On the other hand, 24 per cent of the college-bound students reported their homes had the necessities but not many luxuries, and 4 per cent reported some difficulty in obtaining the necessities, while among job seekers these proportions were 40 per cent and 14 per cent respectively. (Proportions of job-seeking and college-bound students reporting the various levels of family income were almost identical to the proportions reporting these levels in 1950, except among farm students.) Among students from the farm in 1961, fewer for all types of plans reported "comfortable" incomes and more reported less than adequate incomes than was true in 1950. In 1950 a high relationship was found between adequacy of family income and college attendance among farm students, particularly among farm boys. In 1961 these differences had become smaller, and were largest among the girls, while in 1950 a high relationship was found among the boys.

BOOKS IN THE HOME

Almost all the high-ability metropolitan boys attended college, and no marked differences were found in number of books in the home between the college-bound students and the few seeking jobs. Among other residence groups, differences in the number of books were found between the job-planning and college-bound students. Students from homes with more than 100 books more often planned to attend college, while those from homes with fewer than 50 more often planned to get jobs. The proportions of students reporting the number of books in their homes remained similar, for each quantity of books specified, to the proportions reported in 1950 among both the college-bound and job-seeking high-ability groups. Approximately half of the college-bound group and a third of the job-seeking group reported more than 100 books in the home. About 10 per cent of the college-bound and 20 per cent of the job-seeking high-ability students reported fewer than 25 books.

FINANCIAL SUPPORT FOR COLLEGE

Approximately 8 per cent of the metropolitan and nonfarm boys planning to attend college reported that their families would pay all their college expenses. Among farm boys this figure was 4 per cent. Among the girls these figures were 16 per cent for the metropolitan and nonfarm girls and 12 per cent for girls from the farm. Approximately twice as many girls as boys planned on having their parents pay all college expenses. Metropolitan and nonfarm students expected their parents to provide a greater share of their college expenses than did students from the farm. Fifteen per cent of the boys and 10 per cent of the girls expected to be completely self-supporting in college.

140

In 1950 approximately 14 per cent of the metropolitan and nonfarm boys, and 8 per cent of the farm boys, expected their parents to pay all their expenses. Among the girls these proportions were 33 and 22 per cent respectively. Thus the proportion of high-ability students expecting their parents to pay all expenses decreased somewhat for boys, and decreased dramatically among the girls, where the proportions in 1961 were only about half those for 1950. At the same time, students planning to be completely self-supporting in college increased from 10 to 15 per cent for the boys, and from 5 to 10 per cent for the girls.

In 1961 the proportion of high-ability students planning to attend college was 14 percentage points greater than in 1950. These additional college-bound students tended to come from less well-to-do families who were unable to provide as much financial support in college. The proportions shifted in 1961 toward a larger group of students finding it necessary to be self-supporting in college, and a smaller group obtaining complete family support. Among the girls this shift was even more striking than among the boys, and the picture for family support in college among the girls was much closer to that among the boys than was true in 1950, when the differences between the sexes were considerably greater.

Asked if they would change their plans and attend college if they had more money, approximately 50 per cent of the high-ability boys and 45 per cent of the high-ability girls planning to get jobs responded affirmatively, falling a little below the figures for 1950 — 60 per cent for the boys and 56 per cent for the girls. The proportions of job-seeking high-ability students who said they would change their plans and attend college if they had more money were considerably higher than the 25 per cent found among the total population of job seekers.

Of the high-ability students who said they would change their plans and attend college if they had more money, approximately two thirds of the boys and half of the girls indicated they would need money enough for all college expenses. Approximately 30 per cent of the boys and almost half the girls said they would need enough to pay for about half their expenses. Fewer than 5 per cent said they would need only enough to pay less than half their expenses. In 1950 about one third of the boys, but half of the girls, said they would need enough to pay all expenses. In 1961 the proportion of boys needing enough to pay all ex-

141

penses increased from one half to approximately two thirds of the group. It appears that more high-ability students did not attend college for financial reasons in 1950 than in 1961, the few giving these reasons for not attending college in 1961 being those who needed much financial aid.

Approximately 10 per cent of the high-ability students planning to seek jobs said they could easily afford to attend college if they wished. Fifteen per cent indicated they could barely afford it if they wished; approximately 40 per cent said it would involve many sacrifices; and over 40 per cent said they could not afford it. The proportion indicating they could easily afford college — 10 per cent — was similar to that of 1950. Fewer students in 1961 — 15 per cent — said they could barely afford college than in 1950 — 25 per cent. A somewhat larger proportion than in 1950 said they could not afford college. These figures indicate that for many high-ability students, lack of money was not the principal factor in their decision not to attend college. These figures do suggest that for this smaller group of high-ability students not attending college in 1961, lack of adequate financing was more often a determining factor than it was for the students not planning on college in 1950.

FAMILY'S ATTITUDE TOWARD COLLEGE

Of the high-ability students planning to attend college, over 80 per cent said their parents wanted them to attend college, and 15 per cent said their parents insisted they go. Boys and girls from the farm made up the smallest proportion of those whose parents insisted that they attend college. Approximately 5 per cent of the college-bound students said their parents were indifferent. These family attitudes reported by high-ability students were similar to those reported by the total sample of college-bound students, and were also similar to attitudes reported by the high-ability college-bound students in 1950.

Practically none of the farm and nonfarm high-ability students who planned on jobs reported that their parents insisted they attend college. However, this family attitude was reported by a small proportion of the metropolitan students seeking jobs: 8 per cent of the boys and 2 per cent of the girls were apparently planning to get jobs in spite of parental insistence that they attend college. Sixty-five per cent of the metropolitan and nonfarm boys and 45 per cent of the farm boys who planned on jobs said their families wanted them to attend college. Among the girls these figures were 40 per cent and 32 per cent respectively. These proportions were considerably higher than those found among the total population of job seekers. The families of these high-ability job seekers appeared to be much more interested in having their children attend college than the parents of the average students who planned on jobs. Parental attitudes appeared to be an important factor in determining whether or not a high-ability student attended college. At the same time, however, over half the students who planned on jobs instead of college reported that their parents wanted them to go to college. Almost none of the boys said their parents were against college, although 7 per cent of the girls who planned to seek jobs did report this attitude.

INFLUENCE OF MARRIAGE ON PLANS

Only 2 per cent of the high-ability college-bound boys and 4 per cent of the high-ability college-bound girls indicated that marriage had influenced their plans for the following year, and practically none of these students planned to get married within the next two years. On the other hand, approximately 10 per cent of the boys and 28 per cent of the girls seeking jobs said that marriage was an important determinant of their post-high-school plans. These proportions were slightly higher than those reported by the entire population of job seekers. Two per cent of the boys and 5 per cent of the girls planning on jobs said they expected to be married shortly after graduation. Another 2 per cent of the boys and 10 per cent of the girls planned to be married during the year following the one in which they graduated from high school. Marriage, therefore, appeared to be a rather slight deterrent to college attendance among the boys, but somewhat more important for the girls. It was, perhaps, an important factor for somewhere between 15 and 25 per cent of the high-ability girls who did not plan to attend college.

13

High-Ability Students from Workmen's Homes

ONE method used in the 1950 investigation to observe the effects of social and cultural conditions on college attendance consisted of holding constant ability and economic background and studying the relationships between other factors and college attendance. Economic level was held constant by selecting only students who came from workmen's homes — those whose fathers were either skilled or unskilled workers. Variation in ability was minimized by including only students who had scores of 120 or above on the ACE, which placed them in the top 18 per cent of high school seniors. By selecting a similar sample from the 1961 class it was possible to describe the 1961 sample and compare it with the similar group of 1950.

COLLEGE PLANS

In 1961 there were 1856 students from the metropolitan and nonfarm areas whose fathers were skilled workmen or factory workers and who scored above 45 on the MSAT (students from the upper 17 per cent of all Minnesota seniors). Of this sample 1369, or 71 per cent, planned to go to college. In 1950 this percentage was 56 per cent, 530 students out of the total sample of 940. As presented in Chapter 5, the total proportion of all high-ability students planning to attend college increased by 14 percentage points, from 67 to 81 per cent. The proportions of high-ability students from workmen's homes going to college increased at approximately the same rate as that for the total sample of high-ability

144

students, and three times as fast as the 5 per cent increase in college attendance for the entire population of high school seniors.

The proportions of high-ability students from workmen's homes with plans to attend college are shown by sex and residence area for both survey years in Table 39. The largest increase was shown by the non-farm boys, of whom 57 per cent planned to attend college in 1950 as compared with 80 per cent in 1961.

Table 39. Percentages of High-Ability Students from Workmen's Homes Who Planned to Attend College

	1950			1961		
	Total Sample	Plan to Attend College		Total Sample	Plan to Attend College	
Area	(N)	N	%	(N)	N	%
		Boys				
Metropolitan	203	146	71.92	436	350	80.28
Nonfarm	271	154	56.83	397	318	80.10
Total	474	300	63.29	833	668	80.19
		Girls				
Metropolitan	205	100	48.78	543	372	68.51
Nonfarm	261	130	49.81	540	329	60.93
Total	466	230	49.36	1,083	701	64.73
		Boys and Girls				
All	940	530	56.38	1,856	1,369	71.45

APTITUDE AND ACHIEVEMENT

Although this sample of students was highly selected on the basis of scholastic aptitude test scores — all having a raw score of 45 or above — there was still for both sexes a significant difference between the mean scores achieved by those planning on college and those with other plans. Among the boys, those planning on college obtained a mean of 53.38 as compared with their noncollege counterparts, who achieved a mean score of 50.45. College-planning girls achieved a mean score of 54.47 as compared with 51.79 for the noncollege girls. Even among this relatively homogeneous group, differences in ability were related to plans to attend college and were similar to those found in the 1950 study. Considerably larger differences were found in this high-ability group between the high school achievement records of the college and the noncollege groups. The mean high school percentile ranks for the

Table 40. Mean High School Percentile Rank for College- and Noncollege-Bound High-Ability Students from Workmen's Homes

	1950		1961	
Category	N	Mean High School Percentile Rank	N	Mean High School Percentile Rank
Boys				
College	300	76.00	522	78.51
Noncollege	174	55.71	186	56.56
Girls				
College	230	85.57	649	85.06
Noncollege	236	80.67	375	76.27
Boys and Girls				
College	530	80.15	1,171	82.14
Noncollege	410	70.08	561	69.74
Total	940		1,732	

college and noncollege groups are shown in Table 40. Large differences occurred among both sexes, but they were considerably greater among the boys. The figures suggest that the increase among those going to college consisted of students with better high school records.

Many of these high-ability students from lower socioeconomic backgrounds achieved their lower grades in high school because of a lack of academic interest, which would result in a decision not to continue academic work in a college or university.

FATHER'S OCCUPATION

Even in a group homogeneous in father's occupation, differences were still found between the students who went to college and those who did not. As in 1950, in 1961 these differences were significant only among the metropolitan girls, of whom 76 per cent of those going to college, as compared with 64 per cent of those not planning on college, came from homes of skilled tradesmen. Twenty-four per cent of the metropolitan girls planning on college, and 36 per cent of those not planning on college, came from homes of factory workers.

EDUCATION OF PARENTS

The educational level attained by both father and mother were significantly related to the plans of high-ability students from workmen's

146

homes for nonfarm boys and girls from all areas. Significant differences in father's education found among students with different post-high-school plans in 1950 were not found for the male metropolitan students in 1961. This change is consistent with the general trend found among metropolitan boys for socioeconomic factors to be less important determiners of college education in 1961 as compared with 1950. The relationship between father's occupation and post-high-school plans for the other groups was similar to that for 1950 except that the over-all level of father's education had increased since 1950. Of the nonfarm boys 32 per cent of the college planners, as opposed to 62 per cent of the noncollege planners, had fathers who had completed no more than an eighth-grade education. Twelve per cent of these college planners had fathers with some college background, as compared with only 2 per cent of those not planning on college. Of the nonfarm girls, 35 per cent of the college-bound, and 50 per cent of those not attending college, had fathers who had completed the eighth grade or less. Eight per cent of the college-bound and 5 per cent of the girls not planning on college had fathers with some college training.

Similar differences were found between the educational levels attained by the mothers of these students. For the nonfarm boys, 15 per cent of the college-bound had mothers with no more than an eighth-grade education as compared with 27 per cent of those with other plans. Twenty-nine per cent of those bound for college had mothers with some college education as compared with 12 per cent of those not planning to attend. For the nonfarm girls, 16 per cent of the college-bound as compared with 27 per cent of the noncollege students had mothers with an eighth-grade education or less, and for those with some college training, the proportions were 25 per cent for the college-bound and 11 per cent for those not planning on college.

FAMILY INCOME

No significant differences were found between college-bound students and others on the reported adequacy of family income. Approximately 60 per cent described their family's circumstances as "comfortable but not well-to-do" and approximately one fourth said they had "all the necessities but not many luxuries." These proportions were very similar

147

to those of 1950, and in 1950 as in 1961 there were no significant differences between students with different post-high-school plans.

SIZE OF HOME

College-bound students in this group tended to come from families with four or fewer people living in the home; and students with other plans, from families containing nine or more. This difference was significant only for the nonfarm girls among whom, for example, 24 per cent of those reporting a total of three people living in their homes planned to attend college as compared with 14 per cent with other plans. On the other hand, of those who reported nine or more persons in the home, 4 per cent planned to attend college as compared with 10 per cent who had other plans. The relationship of the number of people in the home to college attendance was slight, and differences were found only at the extremes of the distribution.

No relationship was found between either the total number of rooms reported in the home or whether the student had a bedroom to himself and college attendance.

A small relationship was found between college attendance and parental ownership of the home. It was significant only for the metropolitan girls of whom 84 per cent of those reporting home ownership planned to attend college as compared with 74 per cent with other plans.

NUMBER OF BOOKS IN HOME

On the basis of number of books in the home no significant differences were found between students planning on college and those with other plans. About one third of the high-ability students from workmen's homes reported more than 100 books in their homes, and about one fourth reported between 50 and 100. Approximately 20 per cent reported between 25 and 50, and slightly over 10 per cent between 10 and 25. About 3 per cent reported fewer than 10 books in the home. In 1950 a consistent and significant difference between college and noncollege planners was found on this criterion. No such differences were found for the 1961 samples.

ATTITUDE TOWARD COLLEGE

Forty-three per cent of the high-ability children of skilled tradesmen and factory workers who were not going to college said they would

148

change their plans and attend if they had more money. Fifty-seven per cent said they would not. In 1950, 53 per cent said they would change their plans and go to college if they had more financial support. Thus the proportion of these able students not attending college for lack of finances significantly (.01 level) decreased between 1950 and 1961. The real change, however, occurred in the total numbers involved rather than in the proportions. In 1950, 940 high-ability students were from workmen's homes, and within this group 165 students said they would change their plans and attend college if they had more money. In 1961 this total group consisted of 1751 students, but because a higher proportion of them went to college, the total number who said they would attend college if they had more money was only slightly higher than in 1950 — 196 students, 63 boys and 133 girls.

Of the students who said they would go to college if they had more money, about half said they would need enough to pay all expenses; about half said they would need enough to pay approximately half their expenses. Less than 2 per cent said they would need only enough to pay less than half. Of the students not planning on college, approximately 10 per cent said they could easily afford it if they wished to attend. Approximately 15 per cent said they could barely afford it, and 40 per cent said they could afford it, but it would involve many sacrifices. Approximately 35 per cent could not afford college. These proportions were similar to those found in 1950, and again suggest that other than financial factors are involved in reasons for not attending college.

A large proportion of the high-ability students from workingmen's homes who were not planning to go immediately on to college did plan to attend at some later time. There were large sex and area differences in the proportions planning to attend college at a later date. Among the boys, approximately 50 per cent of those from the metropolitan area and 35 per cent of those from the nonfarm area reported plans for attending college after a year or more. Among the girls these proportions were 25 per cent from the metropolitan area and 12 per cent from the nonfarm area.

FAMILY ATTITUDES TOWARD COLLEGE
Over 80 per cent of the college-bound students reported that their parents wanted them to attend college. An additional 13 per cent of the

boys and 4 per cent of the girls reported parental insistence that they attend college. None of the boys and only 1 per cent of the girls reported that their parents insisted that they go, but approximately 65 per cent of these boys and 50 per cent of the girls reported that their parents wanted them to attend. About a third of the boys and over two fifths of the girls not planning to attend college reported their parents were indifferent to their going to college. About 5 per cent of the girls' parents did not want them to attend college. The proportions of college-bound students reporting parental indifference were less than 5 per cent for the boys and about 10 per cent for the girls. Though parental attitudes were important in deciding whether or not these students attended college, they were not all-important, as evidenced by the fact that two thirds of the boys and half of the girls not planning on college reported that their parents wanted them to attend.

EFFECT OF MARRIAGE ON POST-HIGH-SCHOOL PLANS

None of the boys with any types of plans and only about 5 per cent of the girls not planning to attend college said they intended to marry shortly after high school graduation. Approximately 4 per cent of the metropolitan boys not planning on college, and 6 per cent of the girls, planned to marry within two years of graduation. The rest of these students either had no definite plans for marriage or at least expected to marry only after several years. Marriage did not appear to be an important deterrent in keeping high-ability students with lower socioeconomic backgrounds from attending college.

· 14

Girls Who Planned to Enter Nursing

OF THE 22,550 girls who reported their post-high-school plans, 1594, or 7 per cent, planned to enter nursing. Other girls in the sample who planned to enter nursing through a four-year college program and gave "college attendance" as their post-high-school plan were not included in this nursing group. The nursing group consisted primarily of girls who planned to enter a school of nursing, either to earn their certificates as registered nurses or to train, without college preparation, in practical nursing.

The proportions entering nursing varied slightly according to residence area, with 5 per cent of the metropolitan girls and 8 per cent of the farm and nonfarm girls making these plans. The proportion of girls entering nursing increased 1 per cent between 1950 and 1961, and this 1 per cent increase occurred equally in each of the residence areas.

ABILITY AND ACHIEVEMENT

The mean scholastic aptitude test score of girls going into nursing was 33.06, placing them midway between the means of those planning to get jobs and those planning to attend college. Percentile ranks were 65 for high school students and 37 for college-bound students. The mean ability level was the same for girls from each of the three residence areas.

Mean high school ranks varied considerably from one area to another, the metropolitan girls having a rank of 56.7, the nonfarm group 61.5, and the farm group 66.7. The mean high school rank for the farm girls was 10 percentile points above that for prospective nurses from the metropolitan areas. The mean high school rank for all girls entering nursing fell about midway between that for girls planning on jobs and

151

that for girls planning on college. Among the total group surveyed, the mean high school rank was 61.8 for girls entering nursing, 47.3 for those planning on employment, and 72.1 for those planning to attend college.

AGE

For girls planning to enter nursing the median age at the time they were surveyed was 17.55, and the percentages of these girls who were 16, 17, and 18 years of age were similar to those obtained for the entire senior class. There were no significant differences between the ages of girls planning on nursing and those with other plans and no significant differences in the ages of girls who planned to enter nursing in the three residence areas.

FATHER'S OCCUPATION

For almost half the girls planning to enter nursing — 49 per cent from the metropolitan area and 43 per cent from the nonfarm area — the father was either a laborer or a skilled tradesman. In 1950, 56 per cent of the metropolitan and 42 per cent of the nonfarm nursing group had fathers in this category. In the 1961 study, 17 per cent of the metropolitan and 27 per cent of the nonfarm nursing group had fathers in a professional or managerial position. Comparable percentages were found in the 1950 study. Among the girls who lived on farms, a larger proportion had fathers actually engaged in farming than was true for any other plan group. With the exception of the farm girls, paternal occupations for girls planning on nursing closely resembled those for students attending business and trade schools and, to some extent, for girls seeking employment.

EDUCATION OF PARENTS

The median educational level achieved by the fathers of girls planning to enter nursing was graduation from high school for the metropolitan area, some high school for the nonfarm area, and completion of the eighth grade for the farm area. Nineteen per cent from the metropolitan, 15 per cent from the nonfarm, and 3 per cent from the farm area had fathers with some college training. Twenty-two per cent from the metropolitan, 37 per cent from the nonfarm, and 66 per cent from the farm area had fathers whose formal education had not gone beyond the eighth grade.

152

The median education of the mothers was graduation from high school for the metropolitan and nonfarm girls and some high school for the farm girls. Approximately 18 per cent of the girls from each of the regions had mothers with some college training. In 1950 these college figures were 19 per cent for the metropolitan, 20 per cent for the nonfarm, and 24 per cent for the farm group. Although the over-all proportion of students with college-trained mothers increased slightly during the eleven-year period, the proportion of girls going into nursing with college-trained mothers significantly decreased during this time. The proportions with college-trained fathers in 1961, on the other hand, increased as compared with the 1950 figures.

FAMILY INCOME

In the same manner that the level of parental education for girls planning on nursing fell between the educational levels for the college and job groups, the type and level of family income for these girls also fell between these two groups. Fifty-five per cent came from homes where wages were the chief source of income, as compared with 35 per cent of the college-bound girls and 65 per cent of the job-seeking girls in the metropolitan area. Family income was derived chiefly from salaries for 30 per cent of these girls from the nonfarm and metropolitan areas as compared with 38 per cent of the college-planning girls and 20 per cent of the job-seeking girls from these areas. Only a small change in type of family income took place for these girls over the eleven-year period, a slightly higher percentage coming from homes of wage earners rather than salary earners.

Twenty-one per cent of the metropolitan and nonfarm and 29 per cent of the farm girls said their homes had the necessities but not many luxuries. As they did regarding parental educational level and type of family income, these girls fell between those planning on college and those planning on jobs. On the socioeconomic scale, girls planning on nursing tended to rank higher than girls planning on jobs, but not as high as the girls planning on college.

SIZE OF HOME

There was little relationship between size of home and the decision to enter nursing. Nursing-bound girls tended to come from smaller

153

homes than the college-bound in the metropolitan area, while in the farm area their homes were larger than those of students making other noncollegiate plans, and about equal in size to those of college-bound students.

CULTURAL STATUS OF HOME

Three per cent of the metropolitan girls, 5 per cent of the nonfarm, and 6 per cent of the farm girls who planned on nursing reported fewer than 10 books in the home. Twenty-seven per cent of the metropolitan, 24 per cent of the nonfarm, and 19 per cent of the farm girls reported more than 100 books. In 1950, 31 per cent of the metropolitan, 18 per cent of the nonfarm, and 13 per cent of the farm girls had more than 100 books in their homes. The proportion reporting over 100 books in the home, therefore, decreased in the metropolitan area and increased in the nonfarm and farm areas. The median number of books in the home was between 50 and 100 for the metropolitan and nonfarm areas, and between 25 and 50 for the farm area.

Significant differences between areas also emerged on the basis of magazines in the home. The *Reader's Digest* was subscribed to by families of 62 per cent of the metropolitan, 58 per cent of the nonfarm, and 49 per cent of the farm girls. *Time* magazine was taken in the homes of 19 per cent of the metropolitan, 15 per cent of the nonfarm, and 6 per cent of the farm girls. Similar differences were found for many other types of magazines. Three different farm magazines were read in over three fourths of the homes of farm girls entering nursing. The families of girls entering nursing subscribed to fewer magazines than those of girls entering college, but to more magazines than the families of girls with other plans.

Families of girls entering nursing were more likely to belong to the PTA than families of students with other plans except college. Parents of 61 per cent of the metropolitan girls entering nursing were members of the PTA as compared with 43 per cent of those who planned on jobs and 74 per cent of those who planned on college. Among the farm girls, 24 per cent of those entering nursing indicated parental membership in the Farm Bureau, as compared with 29 per cent of those bound for college and 18 per cent of those with other plans. More girls entering nursing had parents who were members of church organizations than

154

those with other plans except the college-bound. Girls entering nursing, then, came from homes of lower cultural status than the college-bound girls, but ranked higher on these indices of home cultural status than students seeking employment or planning to attend other types of schools.

EDUCATIONAL BACKGROUND AND PLANS

Approximately 60 per cent of the metropolitan and nonfarm and 52 per cent of the farm girls planning to enter nursing took a college-preparatory curriculum in high school. This represents an increase of 5 percentage points in each area over the percentage of nursing girls who took a college-preparatory curriculum in 1950. Nine per cent of the girls entering nursing took a commercial course in high school, a decline from the 12 per cent who took a commercial course in 1950. The proportion taking a general course also decreased somewhat in 1961 as compared with 1950. In giving their reasons for taking this curriculum, almost three fourths checked "Fitted vocational plans best," and about one fourth said it was the "most interesting." Twenty-two per cent checked "Parent's advice" as an important reason, and 20 per cent — over twice that of 1950 — checked "Counselor's advice."

The reason most often given for planning on nursing school was to prepare for a vocation. Girls entering nursing checked "to make more money" as a reason for their choice less often than the other students in the survey, whatever their plans. Girls apparently decided to enter nursing without the idea of making much money. They also checked the desire for independence less often than other students except those going to college. Seven per cent said they planned to attend college at a later date. Three per cent said they planned to attend after one year, and 3 per cent after three years.

ATTITUDE TOWARD COLLEGE

Fifteen per cent of the girls planning to enter nursing in 1961 said they would change their mind and attend college if they had more money. This proportion was lower than that for girls planning to enter other types of schools, such as business or trade school, and considerably lower than that for girls planning to seek jobs. In 1950 the proportion who would attend college if financially able was over twice as high — almost 40 per cent — as in the present study. Far fewer girls seemed to be entering nursing as a less desirable alternative to college in 1961 than was true in 1950.

Thirty-six per cent of the girls who said they would go to college if they had more adequate financing said they would need enough money to pay all their expenses, and 56 per cent said they would need enough to pay about half their expenses. In 1950 the proportion needing enough for all college expenses was 31 per cent, a change perhaps due to the increase in students attending college in 1961, with those not going likely to need more assistance. This hypothesis is further supported by the number of girls indicating they could easily afford to go to college if they wished to, which was reported in 1961 by 21 per cent of the metropolitan, 17 per cent of the nonfarm, and 11 per cent of the farm girls. In 1950 this proportion was 18 per cent of the metropolitan and nonfarm girls, and 24 per cent of the farm girls. About 25 per cent of the nursing-bound girls in 1961 said they could not afford college, a proportion similar to that in 1950. In 1950 many girls who wanted to enter college, but could not afford to, entered nursing instead. The proportion of such students was smaller in 1961.

FAMILY'S ATTITUDE TOWARD PLANS

Sixty-eight per cent of the metropolitan and farm girls and 76 per cent of the nonfarm girls entering nursing said their parents wanted them to attend college. Approximately a fourth of the metropolitan and farm girls and a fifth of the nonfarm girls said their parents were indifferent as to whether they attended college. There was no alternative in this item for the girls to check whether their parents wanted them to enter college or some other type of training program, such as nursing, so it is not possible to tell what proportion of these girls were entering nursing when their parents wanted them to attend college. It is apparent, however, that at least for some girls entering nursing, their parents would have preferred that they attend college.

INFLUENCE OF MARRIAGE ON PLANS

Ten per cent of the girls who decided to enter nursing said that marriage had influenced their plans; this percentage was the same across all regions, and lower than that for all other plans except college. As for all plan groups except college, the percentages ran from 15 to

25 per cent. In response to the question "When, in your present plans, are you thinking of marriage?" almost none were at present married, and almost none planned to marry immediately upon graduation. Only 2 per cent planned on marriage during the second year after graduation from high school. About 40 per cent said they were not planning on marriage for a few years, 50 per cent could not say, and 8 per cent were not considering marriage. The proportion who could not say, who had no particular marriage plans, was higher than that for all other groups except those bound for college. The proportion planning on marriage "in a few years" was higher than that for girls going to college. Since these girls planning on nursing seemed to have more definite plans for marriage, perhaps one of the reasons for deciding on a three-year nursing program rather than a college degree was that it could be completed in three years rather than four. Another explanation, of course, may be that girls going into nursing tend to come from a slightly lower socioeconomic level than girls planning on college, and within lower socioeconomic levels there is a tendency to marry at an earlier age.

15

Girls Who Planned to Attend Business School

GIRLS planning to attend business school numbered 1655, or 7 per cent of the senior girls who completed questionnaires. Although the actual number increased from 1015 in 1950 to 1655 in 1961, the proportions of girls planning on business school dropped slightly from 8 to 7 per cent. Distribution among residence areas was as follows: 9 per cent of the farm girls, 8 per cent of the nonfarm girls, and 6 per cent of the metropolitan girls. While the proportions of students planning on college and trade school have increased significantly over the past decade, the proportion planning to attend business school has decreased slightly. A total of 368, or 2 per cent, of the boys planned to attend business school, a proportion similar to that reported in 1950. Because the proportion of boys planning on business school represents only a small share of the total boys graduating, a detailed description of the students planning on business school will be provided only for the girls.

AGE

The median age of girls planning on business school, 17.6 years, did not vary significantly from median ages for girls in most of the other plan groups. Eighty-five per cent were seventeen years old, 11 per cent were eighteen, and 2 per cent were sixteen at the time the questionnaires were completed.

ABILITY AND ACHIEVEMENT

The mean ability level of the girls planning on business school varied slightly according to residence area. The mean MSAT score for those

158

from the metropolitan area was 26.17; from the farm area, 27.38; and from the nonfarm area, 28.18. Thus in terms of average scholastic aptitude the brightest came from the nonfarm areas, the least bright from the metropolitan areas. These scores gave them a percentile rank of 29 among students entering college in Minnesota and of 50 among high school seniors. The mean scores fell well below those for college-bound girls, slightly below the means of girls planning to enter nursing, and above the means for girls planning on trade school or employment.

The mean high school rank for these girls varied considerably by residence area: for the metropolitan area, 47.6; for the nonfarm area, 53.6; and for the farm area, 57.6. Girls with the best high school records tended to come from the farm, the poorest from the metropolitan areas. The pattern was different from that recorded for ability levels. While the mean ability level of the farm girls was below that of nonfarm girls, the farm girls achieved significantly higher records in high school. On mean high school rank, girls planning on business college again fell below college- and nursing-bound students and above those planning on trade school and employment.

FATHER'S OCCUPATION

Fourteen per cent of the metropolitan girls bound for business school had fathers in professional or managerial occupations, as did 23 per cent of the girls from the nonfarm area. Twenty-one per cent of the metropolitan and 24 per cent of the nonfarm girls had fathers who were laborers or factory workers. Thirty-six per cent of the metropolitan girls and 25 per cent of the nonfarm girls had fathers in the skilled trades. The nonfarm girls tended to come from a higher socioeconomic level than those from the metropolitan area. Fathers of girls planning on business school tended to be higher on the occupational scale than fathers of those seeking employment, but considerably lower than fathers of those with college plans and slightly lower than fathers of those entering nursing. Over the intervening eleven years proportionately fewer girls with fathers who owned or managed a business, and more girls with fathers in the skilled trades, attended business school.

EDUCATION OF PARENTS

For girls planning on business school, the median educational level of fathers was graduation from high school for the metropolitan group,

159

some high school education for the nonfarm group, and completion of the eighth grade for the farm group, resembling paternal median levels for all students in each area. Of the girls bound for business school 25 per cent from the metropolitan, 45 per cent from the nonfarm, and 66 per cent from the farm area had fathers with no more than an eighth-grade education. The median education of mothers was graduation from high school for the metropolitan and nonfarm groups, and some high school for the farm group. Fathers and mothers of these girls tended to have less education than parents of girls planning on college, but more education than those of students planning to seek employment. Few of these girls had parents who had attended business school, and there was no more tendency for the daughter of a parent who had attended business school to attend business school herself than to make other plans. In fact, there was a slight tendency for girls whose mothers had attended business school to be more likely to attend college, and in the metropolitan area girls whose fathers had attended business school were as likely to prefer a trade school for themselves. In parental educational levels, these girls tended to be slightly above metropolitan girls seeking employment, considerably above nonfarm and farm girls seeking employment, and similar to the girls — few in number — planning to attend trade school.

FAMILY INCOME

For 62 per cent of the metropolitan girls planning on business school, source of family income was wages; for 23 per cent, salaries. For the nonfarm group these proportions were 51 and 22 per cent. The trend over the eleven-year period was for girls planning on business school to come in increasing proportions from families where wages rather than salaries were the chief source of income. Of these girls 62 per cent reported their families as "comfortable but not well-to-do." An additional 22 per cent said their family income was enough to provide the necessities but not many luxuries. Family incomes appeared to be similar to, but slightly above, the family incomes of students planning on employment, and substantially below those of college-bound students. Business-school girls reported slightly less adequate family incomes in 1961 than girls with similar plans in 1950.

160

SIZE OF HOME

Metropolitan girls planning on business school less often came from homes with only three, four, or five rooms than girls planning on employment. They came from homes with five to seven rooms more often, and from homes with eight or more rooms less often, than girls planning on college. The nonfarm girls less often than college-bound girls came from larger homes with eight or more rooms. Those from the farm came from homes as large as those planning on college did, but more often came from homes with eight or more rooms than girls seeking jobs. More often than the girls with other plans except college, they reported having a bedroom to themselves. No differences in the number of people living at home occurred between business-school girls and those who planned on other types of post-high-school activities.

CULTURAL STATUS OF HOME

Girls planning on business school reported more books in the home than girls planning to seek employment, and fewer books than those who planned to go to college. Of the metropolitan girls, 17 per cent reported fewer than 25 books in the home, as compared with 23 per cent of those seeking jobs and 7 per cent of those going to college. These differences were constant for all residence areas. In each of the areas the number of books reported in the home, although falling between the numbers reported by job-seeking and college-bound students, was much closer to the former. One fourth of the metropolitan girls and 14 per cent of the nonfarm and farm girls reported more than 100 books, and these proportions were almost identical to the proportions of 1950.

The families of girls going to business school were somewhat more likely than families of job seekers, and much less likely than families of students bound for college, to take a particular magazine. In the metropolitan area *Time* magazine was taken by 14 per cent of the families of business-school girls, as compared with 13 per cent for the job seekers and 31 per cent for the college planners. For *Life* magazine, the same proportions were 35, 32, and 44 per cent respectively. One exception was the *Reader's Digest*, the business-school girls falling midway between the job seekers and college-bound students. Among all girls except those from farms these proportions were 51 per cent for business

161

school, 42 per cent for job seekers, and 66 per cent for the college-bound students. These differences were similar across the residence areas, although in almost all cases a higher proportion of metropolitan families took the magazines than nonfarm families, and more nonfarm than farm families. These differences were not present for magazines like *True* and *Argosy*, or for the farm magazines.

Fewer of the girls planning on business school reported parents belonging to organizations than the college-planning girls, while girls seeking employment had the smallest percentage for these three groups. Forty-seven per cent of nonfarm girls going to business school, 35 per cent of the job seekers, and 57 per cent of the college-bound girls reported their parents belonged to the PTA. For church organizations these proportions were 56, 48, and 69 per cent respectively. Organizations for which these differences did not occur included labor unions and veterans' groups.

In cultural status of the home, then, the girls planning on business school fell between the college-bound and the job-seeking girls but were closer to the latter.

REASON FOR PLANS

Approximately 60 per cent of the girls planning on business school took a commercial curriculum in high school, 25 per cent took a general course, and 10 per cent a college-preparatory course. As would be expected, the proportion taking a commercial course was larger than for girls with other plans, but not much higher than the 56 per cent of girls planning on jobs who also took this curriculum. The reason most often given for taking this course was that it best fitted vocational plans, the response checked by 60 per cent of these girls. Thirty per cent said it was the course most interesting to them, and 20 per cent said they did their best work in this type of course. Twenty-two per cent said they were influenced by their parents' advice, a reason checked more often by these girls than by those with any other post-high-school plan except college.

The reason most often given for the decision to attend business school was to prepare for a vocation, checked by 73 per cent of the girls. The reason next most often checked was that it would enable them to make more money, and there were large regional differences in responses to this item. It was checked by 28 per cent of the metropolitan, 34 per cent of the nonfarm, and 40 per cent of the farm girls bound for business school.

ATTITUDES TOWARD COLLEGE

About 20 per cent of the girls from each of the residence areas planning to attend business school said they would change their plans and attend college if they had more money. In 1950 these percentages were 30 per cent for the metropolitan girls and 46 per cent for the nonfarm and farm girls. The proportion of girls who chose business school as a less desirable alternative because they could not afford college was therefore considerably smaller in 1961 than in 1950. Of those in the nonfarm area who said they would attend college if they had more money, about 39 per cent said they would need enough to pay all college expenses, about 54 per cent said they would need enough money for about half, and about 8 per cent enough for less than half their expenses. These figures were relatively constant across residence areas. In 1950, 31 per cent said they needed enough money for all expenses, and 62 per cent enough for about half their expenses. These figures suggest that fewer of the girls bound for business school were not attending college in 1961 because of financial reasons than was true in 1950, but for the smaller group who wanted to but were not able to attend college greater financial assistance was needed in 1961 to enable them to attend.

Saying they could easily afford college if they wished to go were 25 per cent of the metropolitan and 13 per cent of the nonfarm and farm girls planning to attend business school. Those who said they could not afford college were 21 per cent of the metropolitan and 31 per cent of the nonfarm and farm girls. Financial factors appeared more often to be a determinant in deciding on business school rather than college if a girl came from a nonfarm or farm area, since most of the girls who were financially able to go to college but who decided otherwise were metropolitan.

Nine per cent of the metropolitan girls planning on business school said they intended to go to college at a later date. Five per cent planned to attend college after an interval of one year and 2 per cent after two years. Among these girls from farm and nonfarm areas, 4 per cent planned to go to college at some later time.

163

FAMILY'S ATTITUDE TOWARD COLLEGE

One per cent of the girls going to business school said their parents insisted that they go to college. Another 56 per cent of the metropolitan and nonfarm groups and 50 per cent of those from the farm said their parents wanted them to attend college. Forty per cent of these girls from each of the areas said their parents were indifferent about their attending college, and 3 per cent of the metropolitan and nonfarm and 7 per cent of the farm girls said their parents did not want them to go to college. The proportion of these business girls reporting that their parents wanted them to attend college exceeded that for girls with any other type of plan, except, of course, those who were in fact going to college. Fewer girls from farms going to business school said their parents wanted them to go to college than girls from any of the other areas, but even among these farm girls 50 per cent said their parents would have rather had them go to college.

INFLUENCE OF MARRIAGE ON PLANS

Twenty-one per cent of the metropolitan girls planning on business school said that marriage or the early prospect of marriage influenced their plans for the coming year. This was considerably higher than the 6 per cent of the college-bound girls but less than the 26 per cent of those planning on jobs. Fifteen per cent of the nonfarm and farm girls planning on business school answered this item affirmatively, as compared with 25 per cent of the girls planning on jobs and 5 per cent of those planning on college. Girls from the metropolitan area going to business school therefore had marriage plans more similar to those of girls getting jobs and less similar to those of girls going to college than did these girls from the farm and nonfarm areas. Two per cent of the girls bound for business school planned to marry within the year of their graduation from high school and 6 per cent during the following year. One per cent of the college-bound girls and 10 per cent of the job seekers planned to marry the year following graduation, the girls entering business school thus falling about halfway between these other two groups on immediacy of marriage plans.

164

16

Boys Who Planned to Attend Trade School

OF THE 22,206 boys completing the questionnaire, 1820 planned to attend trade school, more than double the 782 boys who indicated this plan in 1950 although the actual proportion of male graduates planning on trade school increased only from 7 to 8 per cent during this period. In addition 979 girls, 4 per cent of the graduating girls, planned to attend trade school, a large increase over the 1 per cent who made this choice in 1950. Since so few of the girls planned to attend trade school, however, no detailed description of them will be provided here.

APTITUDE AND ACHIEVEMENT
The mean MSAT score for boys planning to attend trade school (23.43) was similar to scores for boys entering the service and planning to seek jobs. The mean high school rank for boys bound for trade school (32.49) was somewhat higher than the means for those seeking jobs and entering military service. Compared with the boys planning on employment, trade-school-bound students were of similar ability but had significantly better high school records.

AGE
The median age of boys planning to attend trade school was 17.6 years at the time they filled out the questionnaire. Though similar in age to those planning on jobs, they were slightly older than those planning to attend college, although as mentioned before, age now has ceased to have any meaningful relation to post-high-school plans.

165

PARENTAL OCCUPATION AND EDUCATION

Thirty-five per cent of the metropolitan boys planning on trade school had fathers in the skilled trades, the highest proportion among all students in the survey. Only 3 per cent had fathers in the professions, and 12 per cent had fathers who owned or operated businesses. The median educational level of the fathers was graduation from high school for the metropolitan, some high school for nonfarm, and an eighth-grade education for the fathers of farm boys. The median educational level of the mothers was graduation from high school for the metropolitan and nonfarm groups and some high school for the farm group. A greater proportion of mothers had graduated from high school but had no further training than was true for students with other plans — fewer had either education beyond high school or less than a high school education. In general, however, the occupational level of the fathers and the educational levels of both parents were similar to those indicated by other boys who planned to get jobs or to enter the military service.

FAMILY INCOME

The sources of family income reported by the boys bound for trade school tended to reflect the occupational classification of their fathers. They reported income from salaries, business profits, and professional fees less often than most other groups, and income from wages more often. Sixty-four per cent of the metropolitan group and 48 per cent of the nonfarm group reported family income from hourly or daily wages. Nine per cent of the metropolitan group and 18 per cent of the nonfarm group reported their family income came from professional fees or profits. Fifty-four per cent of the metropolitan and nonfarm boys reported their families to be "comfortable but not well-to-do," and 26 per cent said they had "all the necessities but not many luxuries." In both source and adequacy of family income, these students again were not significantly different from those seeking jobs or entering military service, although in coming more often from lower socioeconomic levels they differed from students selecting other types of post-high-school education.

ATTITUDES TOWARD COLLEGE

Asked whether they would change their plans and attend college if they had more money, 22 per cent of the boys planning on trade school

166

answered affirmatively, a proportion similar to that among boys planning on business school or on other types of post-high-school education. Fifteen per cent said they could easily afford college if they wished to attend, and 25 per cent said they could barely afford college. There were no significant differences between the residence areas on responses to this item. Boys going to trade school differed from those getting jobs and joining the service, however, of whom 30 per cent said they would attend college if they could afford it.

Three per cent of the boys planning on trade school were apparently doing so in spite of parental objections, in that they said their parents "insisted" that they go to college. From the metropolitan and farm areas 54 per cent, and from the nonfarm area 66 per cent, said their parents wanted them to attend college. Some, but perhaps not all, of these parents would have preferred college rather than a trade school for their sons. Parents of 40 per cent of the metropolitan and farm boys and of 28 per cent of the nonfarm boys in the group were reported to be indifferent as to whether their sons went to college.

SIZE OF HOME

No differences in number of rooms in the home occurred among the boys planning on trade school and those who planned either on employment or military service. When compared with students going to college, those planning on trade school more often came from homes with six rooms or less, and less often from homes with nine or more rooms. Among the metropolitan boys 16 per cent of those bound for trade school, and 12 per cent of those bound for college, came from five-room homes. On the other hand, 11 per cent of the college-bound metropolitan boys, and 5 per cent of those going to trade school, came from homes with eleven rooms or more. Similar differences occurred among the metropolitan and nonfarm groups, but not among the farm students.

Similar differences were found in the numbers of persons with whom these students shared a bedroom at home. Of the metropolitan and nonfarm boys 59 per cent of the college-bound had a bedroom to themselves, as compared with 50 per cent of the boys from these areas who were going to trade school, 11 per cent of whom shared their bedroom with two others, as did only 6 per cent of the college-bound boys. Again, these differences occurred only in the metropolitan and nonfarm areas, not among boys from the farm. Although there was a slight tendency for more boys planning on trade school from the metropolitan and nonfarm areas to report eight or more persons living in the home as compared with those planning on college, in general there were few differences among students with various plans on the item dealing with the number of people in the home.

BOOKS AND MAGAZINES IN THE HOME

Four per cent of the metropolitan boys bound for trade school reported fewer than 10 books in their home. Sixteen per cent reported 10 to 24 books, 26 per cent 25 to 49 books, 27 per cent between 50 and 100 books, and 25 per cent over 100 books. The proportion reporting fewer than 10 books (4 per cent) was smaller than the corresponding proportion of job seekers (7 per cent). Otherwise, on number of books reported, boys planning to attend trade school did not differ from those planning on jobs or military service, but reported considerably fewer books than boys bound for college. Thirty-eight per cent of the nonfarm college-bound boys reported over 100 books as compared with 17 per cent of those planning on trade school. Metropolitan trade-school boys had significantly more books in the home than those from nonfarm and farm areas.

For the majority of the magazines listed on the questionnaire, more boys going to trade school than job seekers indicated that the listed magazine was taken in their home, although they did not have nearly the number of magazines found in the home of the typical college-bound boy. The *Reader's Digest* was checked by 49 per cent of the trade-school boys, 45 per cent of those seeking employment, and 64 per cent of those going to college. Among the nonfarm boys, *Time* was checked by 10 per cent of the trade-school group, 8 per cent of the job seekers, and 21 per cent of those planning on college. Magazines like *Popular Mechanics* and *Popular Science* were checked more often by trade-school-bound boys than by any others, while *True* and *Argosy* were checked more often by job seekers than by those going to trade school.

MEMBERSHIP IN ORGANIZATIONS

Boys bound for trade school reported their parents belonged to the organizations listed on the questionnaire slightly more often than boys

168

who planned to get jobs. They less often reported parental membership in organizations than the college-bound boys. Forty-one per cent of the metropolitan, 33 per cent of the nonfarm, and 47 per cent of the farm boys planning on trade school reported parental membership in the PTA as compared with about 34 per cent of those seeking jobs from each residence area. Sixty-four per cent of the college-bound boys from the metropolitan area and 55 per cent from the nonfarm and farm areas indicated their parents were members of the PTA. Parents of college-bound boys were more likely to belong to all types of organizations listed except labor unions than were the parents of boys bound for trade school. In all residence areas church organizations were more often checked by trade-school boys than by boys who planned on jobs. There were a number of differences between residence areas in terms of the organizations to which the parents of boys bound for trade school belonged. The metropolitan parents more often belonged to labor unions and other organizations not listed on the questionnaire. Nonfarm parents were more likely to belong to veterans' organizations, neighborhood clubs, country clubs, and the American Automobile Association. Farm parents were more likely to belong to a farm organization, the ladies' aid, and church groups.

MARRIAGE PLANS

Marriage, or the early prospect of marriage, had influenced the plans of 9 per cent of the metropolitan, 9 per cent of the nonfarm, and 6 per cent of the farm boys who planned to attend trade school, in each case a slightly smaller proportion than for the job seekers and a considerably larger one than for the college goers. For more than 90 per cent of the trade-school boys, then, marriage had not influenced their plans: 1 per cent of those from the nonfarm area were already married, and 1 per cent from the metropolitan area were planning to marry within the coming year. Otherwise, almost none of the boys planning on trade school were thinking about marriage until at least a year after graduation from high school. Even during this second year after graduation only 2 per cent of these boys from each of the residence areas had these plans. Twenty-seven per cent planned to marry in a few years, and 55 per cent had not considered when they might get married. These proportions were similar for all residence areas.

169

EDUCATIONAL BACKGROUND AND PLANS

In high school the boys planning to attend trade school usually took either a shop or a general course, and were more likely to take a shop course than students with any other plan. Metropolitan and nonfarm boys in this group were about equally split between shop and general courses, with 40 per cent in each, while 5 per cent took a commercial course, and 11 per cent a college-preparatory course. Of those from the farm, 28 per cent took the shop course and 44 per cent the general course. Ten per cent took a college-preparatory course, only 3 per cent a commercial course, and 11 per cent an agricultural course. In checking the reasons why they chose their particular program, they more often responded "was best in this work" than students with other plans. The two responses next most often given were "fitted vocational plans best," checked by 43 per cent, and "course seemed most interesting," by 34 per cent.

The reason most often checked for their decision to attend a trade school, "to prepare for a vocation," was given by 75 per cent; the next most popular reason, given by 35 per cent, was that it would enable them to make more money.

Only 12 per cent of these boys planned to attend college at some later date, in contrast to 28 per cent of those getting jobs and 35 per cent of those entering military service. Five per cent said they intended to enter college after one year, 4 per cent after two years, 1.5 per cent after three years, and 1.5 per cent after four or more years.

Of the boys planning on trade school who lived on farms, 60 per cent said they had a major responsibility for a part of its management while in high school, and 49 per cent said there was a place for them in the operation of the family farm which would provide them a good future if they wished to stay.

17

Boys Planning to Enter Military Service

IN 1950, 6 per cent of the male graduates planned to enter military service immediately. In 1961, this proportion, 18 per cent, was three times as great, second only to the proportion planning on college, and greater than the proportion planning on jobs.

APTITUDE AND ACHIEVEMENT
The mean MSAT score for students entering military service (24.64) was well below that for students planning on college but close to, although significantly higher than, the means for boys planning on jobs or trade school. The mean high school rank (31.3) was lower than that for boys planning to attend trade school and equal to that of the job seekers. Aptitudes of boys entering military service, then, tended to be slightly above those of boys with the other two noncollege plans, although they had not attained a high school record equivalent to this ability. In other words, boys entering military service were more likely to be underachievers in high school than boys with other plans.

AGE
As was true of the groups not bound for college, the group entering military service tended to be a little older, having a slightly smaller proportion of seventeen-year-olds and a slightly larger proportion of eighteen-year-olds than the college-bound group.

FATHER'S OCCUPATION
In level of father's occupation boys entering military service generally were similar to students who planned on either employment or trade school with a few notable exceptions. The proportions having fathers in

171

the professions were the same. Compared with the job-seeking group, more fathers of prospective military men were in managerial, sales, or office work, and fewer in skilled trades or laboring occupations, though the differences were slight, so that only a few more students in the military group came from white-collar backgrounds.

EDUCATION OF PARENTS

In educational level of parents the military group was again similar to the job-seeking group — reporting only a few more parents who had graduated from high school or whose education had continued beyond high school — but fell below the students who planned to attend college. The median level of fathers was graduation from high school for the metropolitan, some high school for the nonfarm, and an eighth-grade education for the farm area. The median level for mothers was graduation from high school for the metropolitan and nonfarm areas and some high school for the farm area.

FAMILY INCOME

The responses describing family income followed the same pattern as the responses describing parents' occupational and educational levels. Compared with the boys seeking jobs, slightly more boys planning on military service reported salaries and slightly fewer reported wages as the source of family income. Sixty-one per cent of the metropolitan group and 51 per cent of the nonfarm group reported family income from wages. More of these service-bound boys, as opposed to those seeking jobs, reported their families as "comfortable" or "well-to-do."

SIZE OF HOME

Students planning to enter military service came from the same size homes as the job seekers, but tended to come from slightly smaller homes than the college-bound students. On the item concerning number of people the student shared his bedroom with, those planning on military service again responded in the same proportions as those planning to seek jobs; 48 per cent of the service-bound boys from the metropolitan and nonfarm areas had bedrooms of their own, as compared with 59 per cent of those planning on college from these areas. The group did not differ significantly from the other plan groups in total number of persons living in the home.

172

CULTURAL STATUS OF HOME

On number of books in the home the group ranked slightly higher than the job seekers, but well below students bound for college. As was true among the other plan groups, large differences occurred among residence areas. Nineteen per cent of the metropolitan, 28 per cent of the nonfarm, and 36 per cent of the farm boys bound for military service reported fewer than 25 books in the home. The group more often reported magazines in the home such as the *Reader's Digest*, the *Saturday Evening Post*, *Time*, and the *Ladies' Home Journal* than students seeking jobs.

Parental membership in organizations was reported considerably more often by this group than by students planning to seek jobs. Among the metropolitan service-bound boys 43 per cent had parents in the PTA, as compared with 34 per cent of those planning on jobs. The organizations reported by these students were generally the same ones checked by students planning on other types of schooling than college. On this variable students entering military service differed considerably from those seeking jobs.

Though similar in socioeconomic level to the job seekers, the military group appeared to be of a higher cultural level. That these service-bound students were on the average a little brighter than those seeking jobs may be attributed to their slightly higher cultural status, or perhaps to a higher ability level in the family. In any event this difference had no effect on the high school achievement levels of these students.

REASONS FOR PLANS

About half the metropolitan and nonfarm boys planning on military service took a general curriculum in high school. About one fourth took a shop or technical curriculum, about one sixth a college-preparatory course, and 7 per cent a commercial curriculum. The proportions taking each of these curriculums were somewhat smaller among the farm students, since over one fifth of them took an agriculture program in high school, but were similar to those found among students who planned to seek employment. Reasons most often checked for deciding on these curriculums were that they fitted vocational plans the best and offered the types of courses in which these boys felt they could do their best work.

173

The reason most often given for deciding on military service, checked by 40 per cent, was to prepare for a vocation, although it was given less frequently by this group than by students with plans to continue their education (75 per cent). The second most popular reason was the desire to be independent, given more often by service-bound metropolitan boys than by metropolitan boys with other plans. To make more money than they otherwise could was checked by a fourth to a third of the students making other plans, but by only 5 per cent of these service-bound boys. They also checked "to please parents or friends" less often than other students.

ATTITUDES TOWARD COLLEGE

A third of the metropolitan boys planning to enter military service said they would change their plans and attend college if they had more money. This was a higher proportion than for any other plan group, three times as great as the 11 per cent for students planning to seek employment. Thirty-three per cent of the nonfarm group also answered this question in the affirmative, a proportion smaller than the 38 per cent of those planning on jobs. Twenty-six per cent of the farm group indicated a preference for college if they had more money, as compared with about an equal number of those who planned on jobs. Entering military service, then, seems to be a popular alternative for boys who might otherwise go to college. Forty-five per cent said they would need enough money to pay all their college expenses, 48 per cent enough to pay half, and 7 per cent enough to pay less than half. A smaller proportion of this group said they could easily afford college if they wished than was true for any of the other plan groups. Of the metropolitan and nonfarm students, 12 per cent said they could easily afford college, and 20 per cent said they could barely afford college. Among the farm students this proportion was smaller, with 9 per cent saying they could easily afford college and 23 per cent saying they could barely afford it.

Large numbers of students entering military service plan to attend college at a later date, more, in fact, than from any other plan group. Large regional differences occurred on this variable among these service-bound boys — 40 per cent of the metropolitan, 31 per cent of the non-farm, and 20 per cent of the farm seniors planned to enter college after their tour of service duty. Similar students with other noncollege plans usually intended to go to college after a delay of one year, while most of those entering the service did not plan on college until after two or more years.

The mean aptitude test scores and high school achievement records of this group are well below those of college-bound students, suggesting that many of these college plans are unrealistic. Even if only a part of these boys do eventually enter college, if they enter at the same ratio for each regional area they will increase the already large regional differences in college attendance, since many more of the metropolitan seniors planned on delayed college entrance.

FAMILY'S FEELINGS ABOUT COLLEGE

Two per cent of the boys planning on military service said their parents insisted that they attend college. Fifty-nine per cent of the metropolitan, 46 per cent of the nonfarm, and 34 per cent of the farm students said their parents wanted them to attend college. These proportions and differences among the residence areas were similar to those for students who planned to get jobs upon graduation.

INFLUENCE OF MARRIAGE ON PLANS

Eight per cent of the metropolitan, 6 per cent of the nonfarm, and 5 per cent of the farm boys who planned to immediately enter military service said that marriage had influenced their plans — smaller proportions than for any other group except those who planned to enter college. Less than 1 per cent of the boys entering military service were already married, and only 1 per cent of the metropolitan boys in the group planned to be married shortly after high school graduation. For each of the regions, 1 per cent planned on marriage the year following that of graduation, and all the rest either did not plan to marry for several years or could not say. These students entering the military service, then, had fewer immediate plans for marriage than the students with other post-high-school plans except those bound for college.

18

Profiles: Who Chooses What Plan?

STUDENTS in Minnesota can be divided into many groups on the
basis of their post-high-school plans. The average student in one group
differs from the average student in other groups in many ways: he
comes from a different family background; he has different abilities;
he has different attitudes and values. These groups are different and
the differences lead to inferences about the influences determining a
student's decisions.

Although these group differences are interesting and stimulate specu-
lation, they should not conceal the diversity prevailing in any one
group. On almost any variable, considering almost any dimension, the
total range within any one group approximates the total range for the
entire group of graduating seniors. The brightest student planning to
obtain a job is not much different in ability from the brightest student
in the total group. The dullest student planning to attend college is not
much different from the dullest student in the total group. Although
the average student planning to attend college comes from a higher
socioeconomic level than the average student planning to enter military
service, among students planning to attend college are many from the
lowest socioeconomic levels and among students planning to enlist are
some from the highest socioeconomic levels.

The differences and similarities among the various plan groups are
confusing but certainly not surprising. When one knows the sex of a
student, the area from which he comes, the socioeconomic and cultural
levels of his family, his scholastic aptitude, his high school achievement,
his attitudes and values, perhaps in nine cases out of ten one can predict accurately whether that student will attend college. Multiple correlation coefficients that exceed .70 without including sex or residence

176

area support this conclusion. But any one of several influences can be the primary influence in shaping a student's plans; for one, it may be his high school achievement; for another, his family's economic level. The total group of students planning to attend college is diversified, varied, and heterogeneous. So is each of the subordinate groups. No one student is typical of his group, and yet, for each dimension, an average can be determined.

The profiles that follow, based on figures or averages for each group, are presented to help teachers and counselors understand students with different post-high-school plans. These profiles will defeat this purpose if they lead the reader to forget the diversity within a group. They may help if the reader remembers that these are speculative descriptions based on means accompanied by great variability.

THE COLLEGE-BOUND STUDENT

The typical college-bound high school senior, a boy rather than a girl, usually comes from a metropolitan or suburban area, seldom from a farm. On a scholastic aptitude test he achieves a percentile rank of 78 for high school students.

Although he may come from a family in which the father is a blue-collar worker, his father is more likely to be in a professional or managerial occupation than the fathers of students with other post-high-school plans. Unless he comes from a farm, both his mother and his father are high school graduates and, in about a third of the cases, have some college experience. If he comes from a farm, his parents have only an eighth-grade education and only seldom has either attended college. In any case, the parents of a college-bound student usually have had more formal education than parents of students in any other plan group. His father is on a fixed salary and is less likely to be paid hourly or daily wages than the other fathers. If the student comes from a farm, his father is primarily a farmer rather than working at something other than farming. He describes his family's standard of living as "comfortable but not well-to-do." He comes from a slightly larger home and is more likely than students with other plans to have a bedroom to himself.

The college-bound student has more than 100 books in his home unless he comes from a farm, in which case he reports between 25 and 50 books. He also has more magazines in his home than the other students,

177

usually the *Reader's Digest,* a household magazine such as *Better Homes and Gardens,* a woman's magazine such as *Ladies' Home Journal* or *McCall's, Life,* and either *Time* or *Newsweek.* If he comes from the farm the magazines are usually the *Reader's Digest* and several farm magazines. His parents also belong to more organizations, are members of the PTA, and belong to a church group. If he is from the city they are members of the American Automobile Association. If he is from the farm his mother is a member of the ladies' aid and his father a member of the Farm Bureau rather than the Farmers Union.

The typical college-bound boy expects to receive financial help from his family to meet some but not most of his expenses. In less than 10 per cent of the cases does he expect his parents to pay all his college expenses and in 15 per cent of the cases he expects no help at all. The college-bound girl expects more financial help from home than the boy.

In high school the typical college-bound student took a college-preparatory curriculum, his reasons being that it fitted his vocational plans the best and that he followed the advice of his parents and his high school guidance counselor. The most important reason he gives for going to college is to prepare for a vocation. That college will enable him to make more money and will give him a liberal education are less often given, though still checked by a substantial number. He also may be planning on some type of graduate or professional training after college — about half the boys had such plans — while girls are unlikely to have them. Neither college-bound boys or girls have any plans for marriage in the near future.

THE GIRL ENTERING NURSING

On a scholastic aptitude test, the typical girl entering nurse's training achieves a percentile rank of 56 for high school students. This places her at the thirty-seventh percentile among college-bound students in the state. Although her ability is the same regardless of residence area, her actual performance in high school varies considerably according to where she lives. If she comes from the farm her high school percentile rank is 67; if from a town or small city, 62; if from a metropolitan area, 57. Her aptitude and ability and achievement levels are below those of girls planning to attend college but above those of girls in all other plan groups. If she comes from a metropolitan area, her father is a skilled tradesman or laborer and graduated from high school; if she comes from a smaller city or town or farm, her father has no more than an eighth-grade education. If she comes from the farm, her mother is likely to have had only an eighth-grade education. If from other residence areas, her mother is usually a high school graduate. Wages are the chief source of family income and she feels that the family is "comfortable but not well-to-do." Still, she gives her family a higher financial rating than the other students give theirs, except the college-bound.

She reports between 50 and 100 books in her home unless she comes from the farm, where there are between 25 and 50. Among the magazines found in her home are the *Reader's Digest, Life* or *Look,* a household magazine such as *Better Homes and Gardens,* and a woman's magazine such as the *Ladies' Home Journal* or *McCall's.* Her parents are members of the PTA and a church organization. If she comes from the metropolitan area, her father is a member of a labor union. If she is from a small town, her father belongs to a veterans' organization and her mother to the ladies' aid. If she is from the farm, her mother is also a member of the ladies' aid and her father is more likely to belong to the Farmers Union than the Farm Bureau.

In high school she took a college-preparatory curriculum; her reason for doing so was that it fitted her vocational plans the best. She is also likely to indicate the advice of parents and guidance counselors as important reasons. Of the various reasons given for her post-high-school plans she checked only "to prepare for a vocation." She would not have changed her plans and entered college if she had had more money. She feels she could more easily have afforded to attend college had she wished to go than students in the other plan groups. Her parents were in favor of her going to college.

The early prospect of marriage did not influence her plans to enter nursing school and she has no plans to be married, at least for several years.

THE GIRL ENTERING BUSINESS SCHOOL

Although she will be attending a business school in a metropolitan area, the girl planning on doing so usually comes from a farm, town, or smaller city rather than a metropolitan area.

179

If she comes from the farm, town, or smaller city she achieves a higher score on the scholastic aptitude test than the metropolitan girls in her group. Her score gives her a percentile rank of 50 for high school seniors and of 29 for college-bound students — well below that of the college-bound girl, slightly below that of the girl planning to enter nursing, and somewhat higher than that of the girl planning to attend a trade school or to seek employment. If she comes from the farm her high school percentile rank is 58; if from a town or smaller city, 54; and if from the metropolitan area, 48. Again, she does less well in high school than the typical girl who plans to go to college or into nursing, but she does better than the students planning on trade school or a job.

Her father is a skilled tradesman or laborer unless, of course, she comes from the farm. Source of family income is hourly or daily wages, and she feels that the family is "comfortable but not well-to-do." She comes from a home that is slightly smaller than that of the girl who plans on college. If she comes from the metropolitan area, her father is a high school graduate and otherwise has an eighth-grade education. He is less likely to have attended a business school than fathers in most of the other plan groups. If she comes from the farm, her mother completed an eighth-grade education and otherwise has a high school diploma. Her mother is no more likely to have attended business school than mothers of girls with other plans.

She reports between 25 and 50 books in her home. Magazines include the *Reader's Digest, Saturday Evening Post* or *Look*, a woman's magazine such as *Ladies' Home Journal* or *McCall's*, and a household magazine such as *Better Homes and Gardens*. If she comes from a farm there will be fewer of these magazines but the family will subscribe to several farm periodicals. Her parents belong to the PTA and a church organization. If she lives in a city her father belongs to a labor union, and if she lives on the farm her parents are members of the Farmers Union rather than the Farm Bureau. If she comes from the farm her mother is a member of the ladies' aid.

She has already received some business training in high school, where she took a commercial curriculum because it fitted her vocational plans the best and she found it the most interesting. She reports her parents helped her in this decision but her high school counselor did not. She is going to business school to prepare for a vocation and because this

180

training will allow her to make more money. Although the typical girl attending business school would not change her plans and attend college if she had more money, a higher proportion of these girls would change their plans if money for college were available as compared with girls in most of the other plan groups. The typical girl going to business college thinks she could have afforded college had she wished to go. In about half the cases she reports that her parents would have liked to have her go to college.

She has no immediate plans to be married, but in a number of instances indicated that the possibility of marriage has influenced her plans for the coming year.

In ability, high school achievement, and socioeconomic and cultural status, the girl planning on business school falls below the girls about to attend college and to enter nursing but above those seeking employment and the few planning to attend a trade school.

THE BOY ENTERING TRADE SCHOOL

Boys planning to attend trade school come in equal proportions from the metropolitan areas, from towns and smaller cities, and from the farm. The typical boy in this group had an MSAT score of 23, giving him a percentile rank of approximately 39 for high school students and 14 for college entrants. His ability level is similar to that of boys planning to seek jobs and to enter military service. His high school rank of 32 is slightly above that for boys with other noncollege plans. Compared with those boys, he is a slight overachiever. His father is likely to be a skilled tradesman; a higher proportion of boys bound for trade school have fathers in the skilled trades than do students with any other type of plan. If he comes from the city his father is either a high school or eighth-grade graduate. His mother is a high school graduate unless he comes from the farm, in which case she has an eighth-grade education.

The family income is from hourly or daily wages, and he describes it as "comfortable." His home is a little smaller than that of the college-bound students. He reports between 25 and 50 books in his home and fewer books and magazines than the student going to college. His family may take the *Reader's Digest* and one or two other popular magazines and is more likely to take *Popular Mechanics, Popular Science,* and magazines of that kind than families of students with other plans. In

181

general the magazines taken in his home reflect more masculine interests. In addition to the mechanical magazines, he is more likely to report *Sports Afield* and less likely to report the *Ladies' Home Journal* and *Good Housekeeping* than are boys with other post-high-school plans. His parents may be members of the PTA and a church organization. If he lives in the city his father belongs to a labor union. If he lives on a farm his mother is a member of the ladies' aid and his father belongs to the Farmers Union rather than the Farm Bureau. His parents are less likely to be members of the American Automobile Association than parents in the other plan groups. With stronger mechanical interests, these families apparently find less need for such services.

He says he would not change his plans and attend college if he had more money. More often than boys with other types of plans, he says he could have afforded college had he wished to attend. He also indicates less often than other students that his parents would prefer that he go on to college.

In high school he took either a shop curriculum or a general curriculum. If from the city he more likely took the shop program; if from the farm he more likely took the general program perhaps because he went to a smaller high school where a shop curriculum was not available. His reasons for taking this program are that it fitted his vocational plans the best, that this course was the most interesting, and that he did his best work in this type of course. He is attending a trade school because it will prepare him for a vocation and will enable him to make more money. He has no plans to attend college at a later date. As with most twelfth-grade boys, marriage did not influence his plans for the coming year.

THE JOB-SEEKING STUDENT

The typical job-seeking student is more likely to be a girl than a boy, and more likely to come from a farm than from a town or city. This student scores lower on the MSAT and has poorer high school grades than students in the other plan groups. The typical boy has a high school rank of 30, the typical girl 47. Parents are either skilled tradesmen or laborers or farmers and are less likely to be in professional or managerial occupations than the parents in the other plan groups. Although the typical student seeking employment reports that his family is "comfortable but not well-to-do," he is more likely to report less than adequate family income than are students with other plans. His father typically completed the eighth grade while his mother graduated from high school if she lived in the city, but she too only completed the eighth grade if she came from the farm.

The student planning to seek employment comes from a slightly larger family and from a home slightly smaller in size than the college-bound student. He usually reports between 25 and 50 books in his home, although more from this group than from any other reported having fewer than 10 books in the home. He also reports fewer magazines than the other students, although the *Reader's Digest* was checked by 40 per cent of the group. He is more likely than the typical college-bound student to have magazines such as *True* and *Argosy* in his home. If he comes from a farm his family receives several farm magazines. His parents, though less likely to belong to organizations than the other parents, are more likely to belong to a labor union than parents of the college-bound, and if he lives on a farm his father is more likely to belong to the Farmers Union than to the Farm Bureau. The parents of the typical job seeker are far less likely than parents of the typical college-bound student to belong to any kind of organization. If the job-seeking student is a boy from the city only rarely does he indicate he would change his plans and attend college if he had more money. Among girls and boys planning on jobs from nonmetropolitan areas, about one in four says he would attend college if financially able to. Almost all say they would need enough money to pay all or at least over half their expenses before they would be able to attend. Nonmetropolitan girls and boys indicate considerably less parental interest in their attending college than students with other post-high-school plans. About one in four of the boys and one in seven of the girls plan to attend college at a later date. The time most often indicated is after staying out of school one year.

In high school, the typical job-seeking boy took a general curriculum, the typical girl a commercial program. Boys occasionally took shop programs, and those living on farms agricultural programs. The typical boy chose his course because he found it the most interesting; the typical girl chose hers because it fitted her vocational plans the best. Job-seeking students are unlikely to indicate that their choice of high school curriculum was influenced by the advice of parents, teachers, or coun-

183

selors. The chance to begin making money quickly and the desire to be independent are the two principal reasons given by the typical job seeker for his choice of plan. Although marriage did not influence the plans of male job seekers, about one in four of the girls indicated that marriage or the early prospect of marriage influenced their plans for the coming year. This is a considerably higher proportion than that for girls who planned on some type of vocational training after graduation.

Students planning to seek employment upon graduation from high school tend to be less able, to have poorer high school records, and to come from families of lower socioeconomic and cultural status than students in the other plan groups.

THE BOY ENTERING MILITARY SERVICE

The boy planning to enter military service is somewhat more likely to come from either a farm or a smaller city rather than the larger urban and suburban areas. On the MSAT he scores slightly higher than the typical boy planning to get a job or attend trade school, and his high school achievement record is only equal to that of boys planning to seek jobs and somewhat below that of boys entering trade school. He tends to be an underachiever in high school more than the typical boy with some other type of plan.

Although his father is usually a skilled tradesman or laborer, the military group had more fathers in white-collar occupations than the other noncollege plan groups. His father is likely to be a high school graduate if he comes from the city and to have an eighth-grade education if from the other areas. His mother has a high school education unless he comes from a farm, in which case she has completed only the eighth grade. His family typically receives its income from hourly or daily wages, although more fathers in this group were on salary than the fathers of students seeking jobs or bound for trade school. He comes from a slightly larger family and lives in a slightly smaller home than the college-bound student. He has between 25 and 50 books in his home, more than the student who takes a job but fewer than the student going to college. The *Reader's Digest* and one or two other magazines are usually found in his home. His family is somewhat more likely to sub-scribe to magazines than that of the job-seeking student but they do not take nearly as many as the family of the college-bound student. His

184

father is more likely to be a member of a labor union than the father of the college-bound student but otherwise his parents are members of fewer organizations. They may belong to the PTA and a church organization, and if living on a farm his mother may belong to the ladies' aid.

He is more likely than other students to report that he would change his plans and attend college if he had more money; he is also likely to plan on attending college at some later date — usually after a period of three to four years. He reports more often than students with other noncollege plans that his parents want him to go to college. In high school he was most likely to take a general curriculum, tending to avoid the more specific programs — college-preparatory, shop, or commercial courses — unless he lived on a farm, in which case he was quite likely to take an agricultural curriculum. He did not check many reasons for his choice of high school curriculum. If he did he usually checked it as the program he found the most interesting. His reasons for choosing military service are either to prepare for a vocation or to be independent. Compared with the job hunter, the student going into military service has slightly more ability and comes from a home that is slightly higher both in socioeconomic and cultural levels. His record of achievement in high school, however, is the same as that for the job-seeking student.

INDEX

Index

Ability: and college plans, 8, 111–13; and socioeconomic variables, 114–15. *See also* American Council on Education Psychological Examination; High school percentile rank; Minnesota Scholastic Aptitude Test

After High School — What? 14

"After High School — What?" questionnaire, 17, 28–33

Age: and college plans, 9; of students in *1950* and *1961* studies, 57; of college-planning students, 116; of work-planning students, 127; of high-ability students, 136; of girls with nursing plans, 152; of girls with business school plans, 158; of boys with trade school plans, 165; of boys with military service plans, 171

Agriculture degrees, decrease in, 43

American Council on Education Psychological Examination, 70: scores of high-ability students, 79, 135; scores and college plans, 111

Andrew, D. C., 18, 25

Aptitude, *see* Ability; American Council on Education Psychological Examination; Minnesota Scholastic Aptitude Test

Arkansas high school students, *1957* study of, 18

Artis, J., 25

Attitudes of parents: of college-planning students, 122–23; of work-planning students, 133–34; of high-ability students, 142–43, 149–50; of girls with nursing plans, 156; of girls with business school plans, 164

Attitudes of students, 38. *See also* Attitudes toward college; Personality inventory

Attitudes toward college: of work-planning students, 132–33; of high-ability students, 148–49; of girls with nursing plans, 155–56; of girls with business school plans, 163; of boys with trade school plans, 166–67; of boys with military service plans, 174–75

Average student, *see* Typical student

Beegle, J. A., 25

Beezer, R. H., 14, 18, 24

Berdie, R. F., 24, 40: on comprehensive high schools, 5; *After High School — What?* 14; quoted, 17; and Minnesota Scholastic Aptitude Test, 33

Books in high school library, and college-planning students, 89–90

Books in homes: in *1950* and *1961* studies, 61; and realizability of plans, 69; of college-planning students, 110, 119; of work-planning students, 130; of high-ability students, 140, 148; of girls with nursing plans, 154; of girls with business school plans, 161; of boys with trade school plans, 168; of boys with military service plans, 173

Bridgman, D. S., 21, 24

Bureau of Labor Statistics, 21

Business school plans: in *1961* study, 37; frequency of, 56, 158; in *1962* follow-up study, 66; and aptitude test scores, 74, 158–59; and high school percentile rank, 78, 159; and age, 158; sex differences in, 158; urban-rural differences in, 158; and parents' occupation, 159; and parents' education, 159–60; and family income, 160; and size of home, 161; and books and magazines in home, 161–62;

Minnesota *1961* study: objectives, 28; "After High School — What?" questionnaire, 28–33; school questionnaire, 33; test scores, 33; student sample, 33–34; school and community sample, 34; groups compared, 34–35

Minnesota *1962* follow-up study, method of, 35–36

Minnesota Scholastic Aptitude Test, 70: and prediction of academic success, 33; scores in *1962* follow-up, 64; scores and realizability of plans, 69; sex differences in scores, 71, 74; urban-rural differences in scores, 71, 74; scores of college-planning students, 74, 111; scores of students with work plans, 74, 126; scores of girls with nursing plans, 74, 151; scores of girls with business school plans, 74, 158–59; scores of boys with trade school plans, 74–75, 165; scores of high-ability students, 79, 103–4, 135; relation of scores to plans, 103–4; scores of boys with military service plans, 171

Moriguchi, C., 21, 25

Mother's occupation, *see* Occupation of parents

Multiple correlations: between socioeconomic variables and college plans, 110–11; between ability measures and college plans, 112; between socioeconomic and ability measures and college plans, 114

National Defense Education Act, counseling provisions of, 28

National Merit Scholarship Program, 21, 43

Nationwide studies, summary of results, 20–22

Needs: definition of, 10; of high school graduates, 10–13

Nelson, T. M., 20, 25

New Mexico, and study of high school students, 17

Nonfarm group, definition of, 35

Nursing plans: frequency of, 56–57, 151; and aptitude test scores, 74, 151; and high school percentile rank, 78, 151–52; and urban-rural differences, 151; and age, 152; and parents' occupation, 152; and parents' education, 152–53; and family income, 153; and size of home, 153–54; and parents' membership in organizations, 154–55; and books and magazines in home, 154; and cultural

status of home, 154–55; and high school curriculum, 155; reasons for, 155; and students' attitudes toward college, 155–56; and family's attitudes, 156; and marriage plans, 156–57; typical student with, 178–79

Occupation of parents: in *1950* and *1961* studies, 57–58; and students' responses on personality inventory, 104; and students' plans, 107–8; of college-planning students, 116–17; of students with work plans, 127; of high-ability students, 136–37, 146; of girls with nursing plans, 152; of girls with business school plans, 159; of boys with trade school plans, 166; of boys with military service plans, 171–72

Ohio Psychological Examination, 33, 70

Organizations, parents' membership in, 61–62, 120–21, 130, 154–55, 162, 168–69, 173

Orr, D. B., 25

Parent-teacher associations, parents' membership in, 62, 93, 120–21, 154, 162, 169, 173

Parents: influence on students, 5, 6, 62, 124, 131, 155, 162; and college plans for children, 21; education of, 21–22, 58–59, 108–10, 117–18, 127–28, 137–39, 146–47, 152–53, 159–60, 166, 172; occupations of, 57–58, 104, 107–8, 116–17, 127, 136–37, 146, 152, 159, 166, 171–72; membership in organizations in *1950* and *1961* studies, 61–62; attitudes of, 68, 122–23, 133–34, 142–43, 149–50, 156, 164, 167, 175; membership in organizations, 120–21, 130, 154–55, 162, 168–69, 173

Personal values, *see* Personality inventory

Personality inventory: construction of, 97, 100; items in, 98–99; sex differences in responses, 100; urban-rural differences in responses, 101; and responses of students with varying plans, 101–3; and responses of high-ability students from low socioeconomic strata, 103–4

Plans: and high school curriculum, 3; general influences on, 5–6; review of research on, 14–22; carried out in *1950* study, 36; carried out in *1961* study, 36–37; correlates of, 37; and MSAT scores, 103–4; of high-ability students, 136. *See also* Business school plans; College